CHICHESTER,
& LITTLEHAM

G000298313

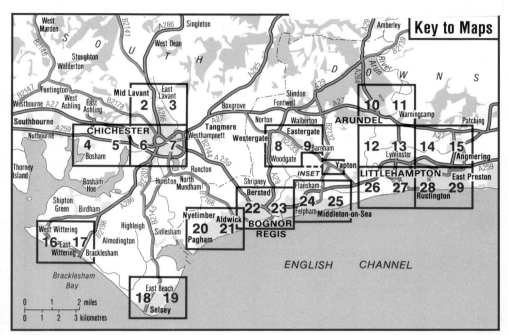

Key to Maps

Reference

'A' Road	A286	Residential Walkway ··········	Ambulance Station ✚
Under Construction		House Numbers A & B Roads only 2 23	Car Park Selected 🅿
Proposed			Church or Chapel ✝
'B' Road	B2178	Railway Level Crossing | Station	Fire Station ■
Dual Carriageway		District Boundary ─ · ─ · ─	Hospital 🄷
One Way Street		Posttown Boundary By arrangement with the Post Office	Information Centre 🄸
Traffic flow on A roads is indicated by a heavy line on the drivers left.	→	Postcode Boundary Within Posttown	Places of Interest Mus.
Pedestrianized Road		Built Up Area	Police Station ▲
Restricted Access			Post Office ★
Track		Map Continuation 10	Toilet ▽
Footpath		National Grid Reference ⁴85	With Facilities for the Disabled ♿

Scale

1:15,840

4 inches to 1 mile

0 ¼ ½ ¾ mile

0 0.5 1 kilometre

Geographers' A-Z Map Co., Ltd.

Head Office : Fairfield Road, Borough Green, Sevenoaks, Kent. TN15 8PP Telephone : 01732 781000
Showrooms: 44 Gray's Inn Road, London, WC1X 8HX Telephone 0171 242 9246

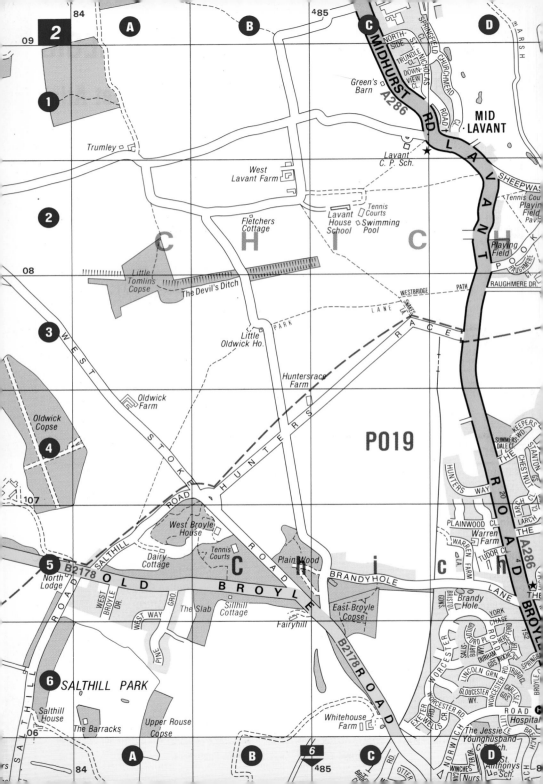

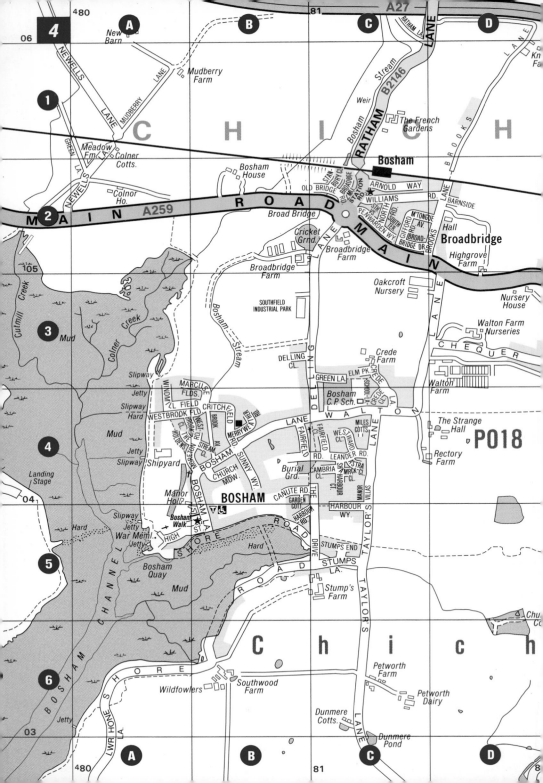

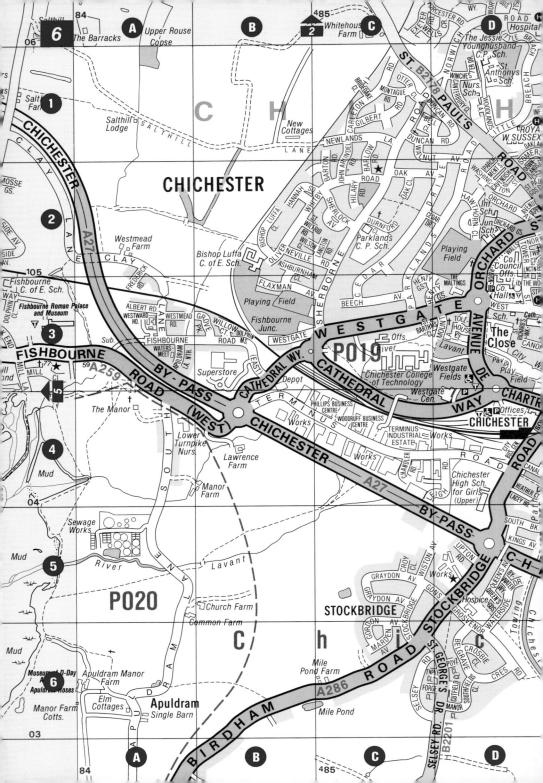

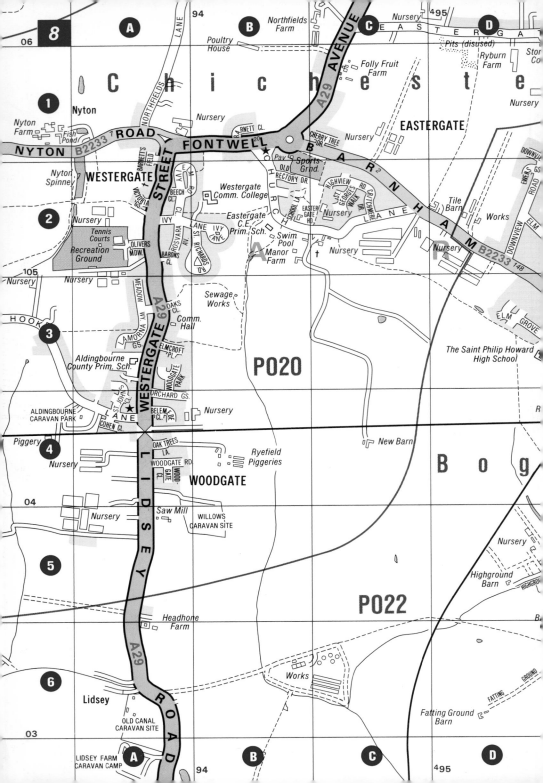

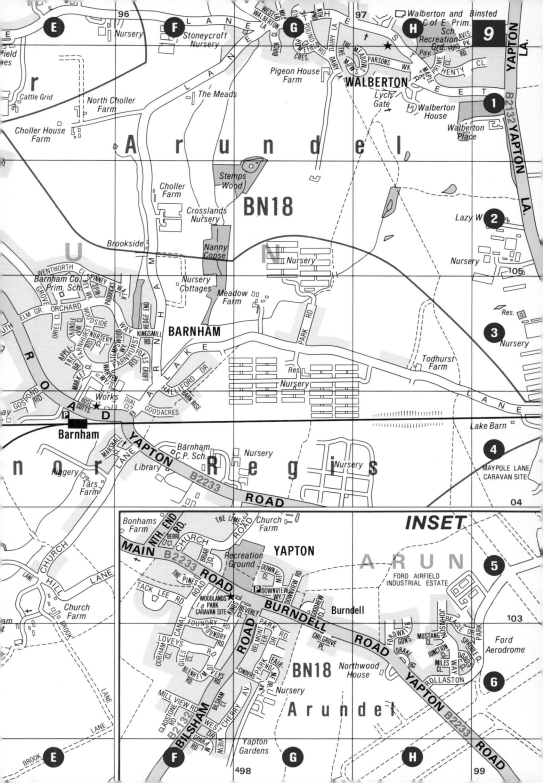

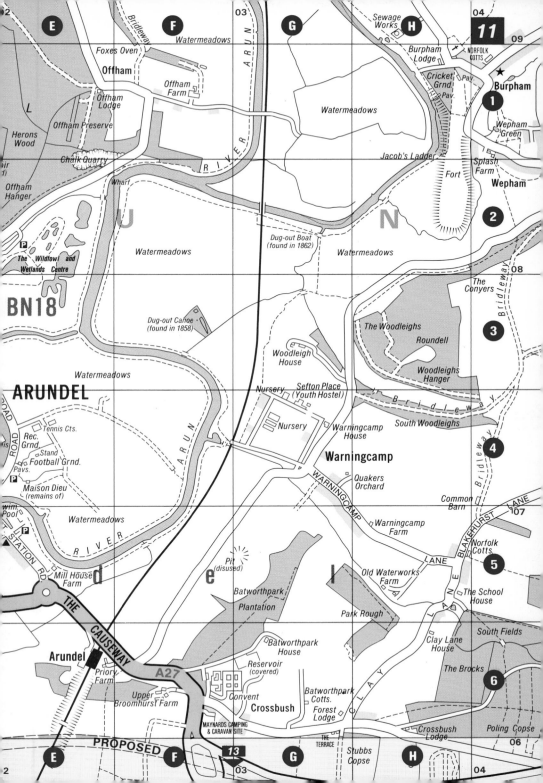

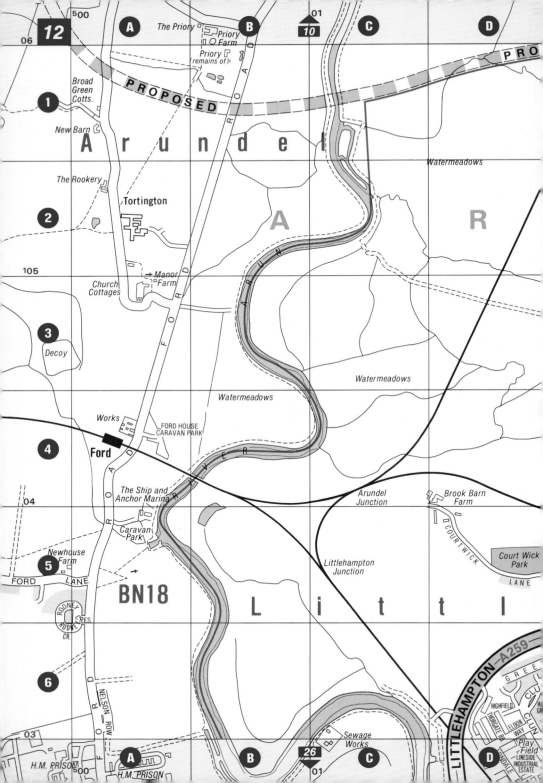

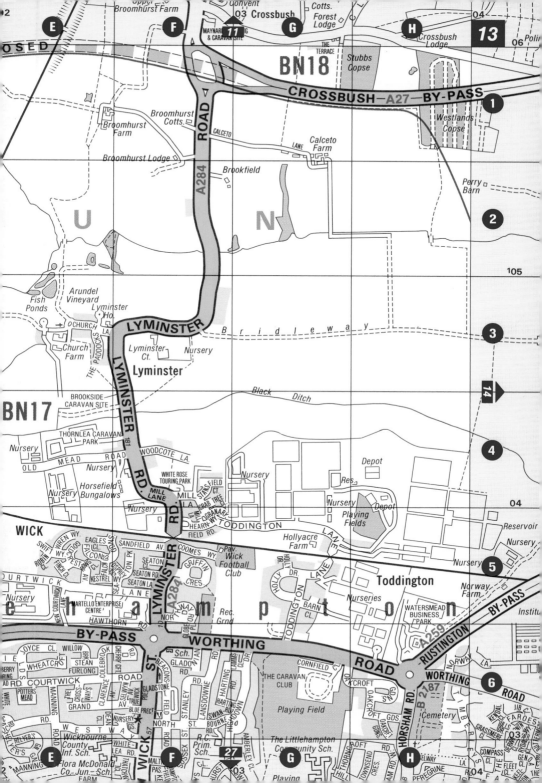

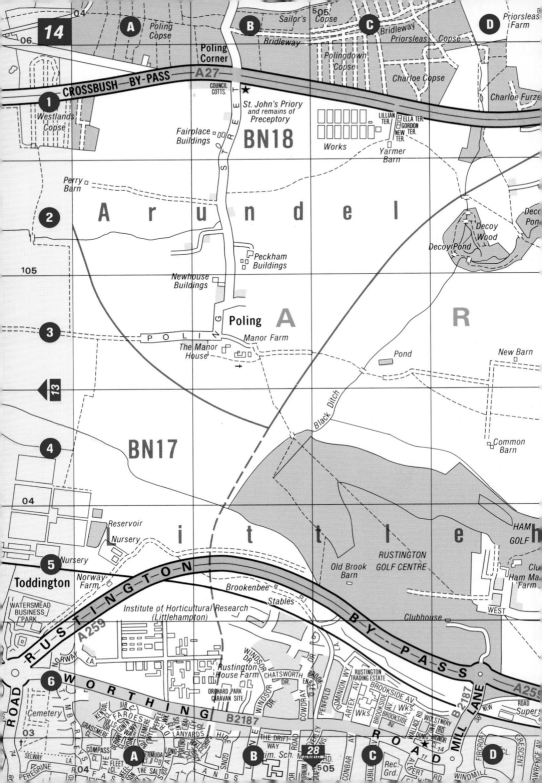

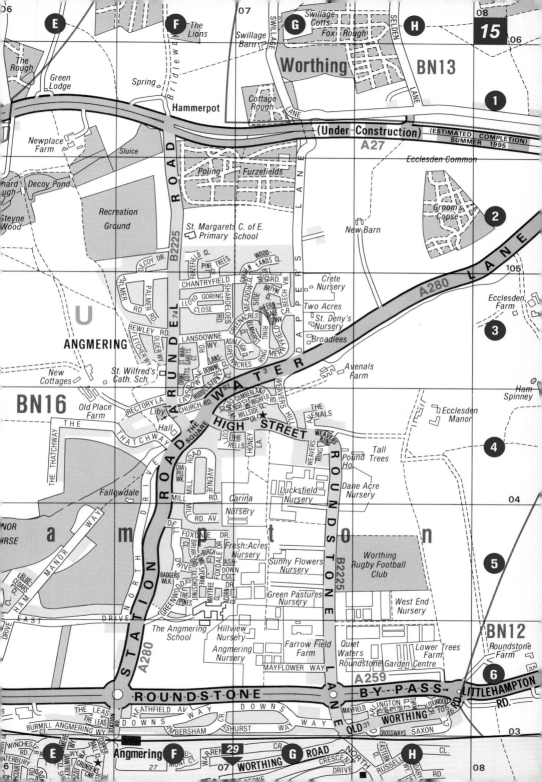

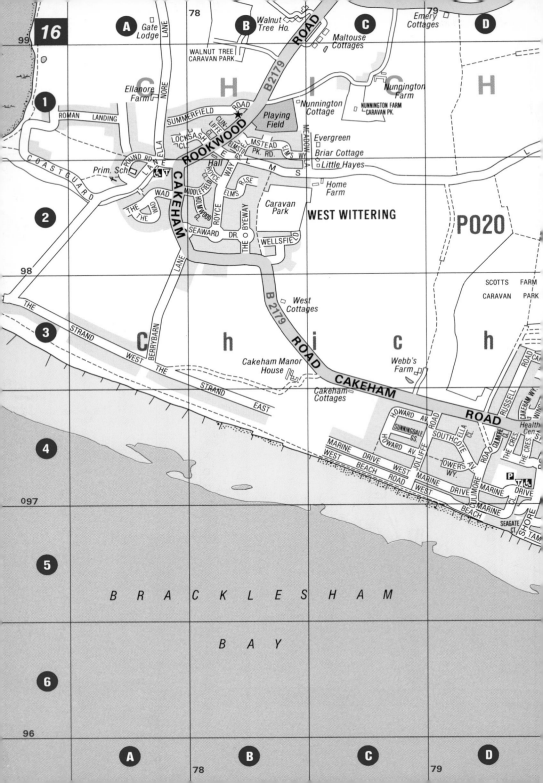

16

99

A Gate Lodge

78 B Walnut Tree Ho. 79 C Emery Cottages D

Maltouse Cottages

WALNUT TREE CARAVAN PARK

B 2179 ROAD

C   H   I   C   H

Ellanore Farm

Nunnington Farm

1 ROMAN LANDING

SUMMERFIELD ROOKWOOD ROAD

Nunnington Cottage

Nunnington Farm CARAVAN PK.

CUNLIFFE

Playing Field

MEADOW

LOCKSASH CL.

ELMSTEAD PK. RD.

ELMS WY.

Evergreen
Briar Cottage
Little Hayes

COASTGUARD

Prim. Sch.

POND RD.

ELLA LANE

CAKEHAM

Hall

ROYCE WY.

ELMS

ELMS

Home Farm

2 THE WAD

MIDDLEFIELD

ROYCE

RISE

Caravan Park

WEST WITTERING

PO20

THE WAD

SEAWARD DR.

HOLMWOOD

THE BYEWAY

WELLSFIELD

LANE

98

West Cottages

B 2179 ROAD

SCOTTS CARAVAN FARM PARK

THE STRAND

3 THE STRAND WEST

BERRYBARN

THE STRAND EAST

C   h

Cakeham Manor House

CAKEHAM

Webb's Farm

C   h

Cakeham Cottages

RUSSELL ROAD

CAKEHAM WY.

Health Cen.

HOWARD AV.

SUNNINGDALE GS.

HOWARD AV.

JOLLIFFE ROAD

SOUTHCOTE AV.

ELLA CL.

CULMORE CL.

THE CRES.
THE CRES.

4

MARINE WEST

WEST BEACH ROAD

WEST DRIVE

TOWERS WY.

MARINE DRIVE

P

MARINE DRIVE

097

WEST BEACH

MARINE CL.

SHORE

SEAGATE CT.

TAM

5

B R A C K L E S H A M

6

B A Y

96

A 78 B C 79 D

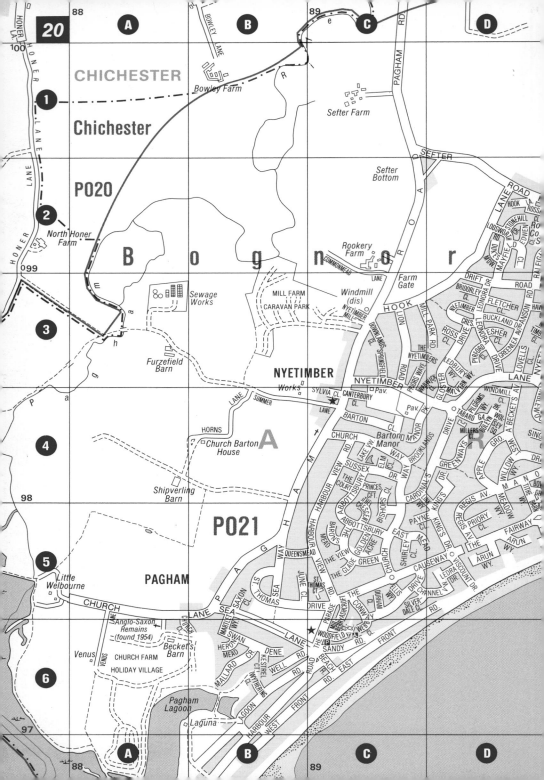

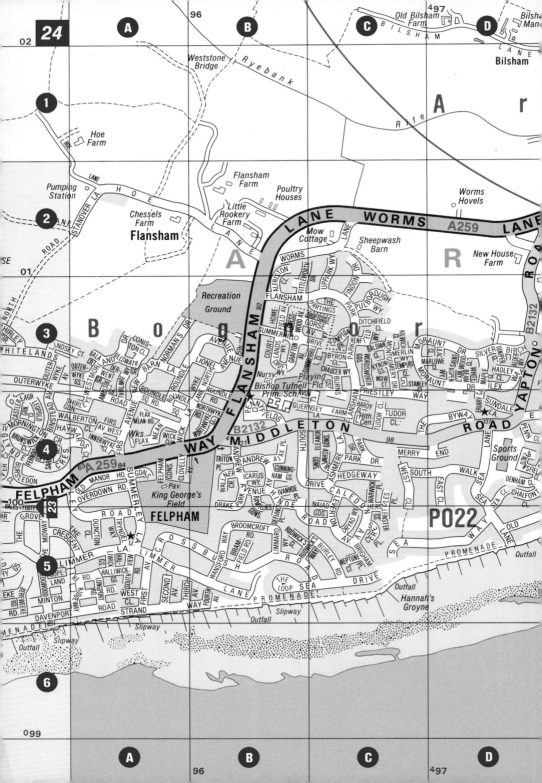

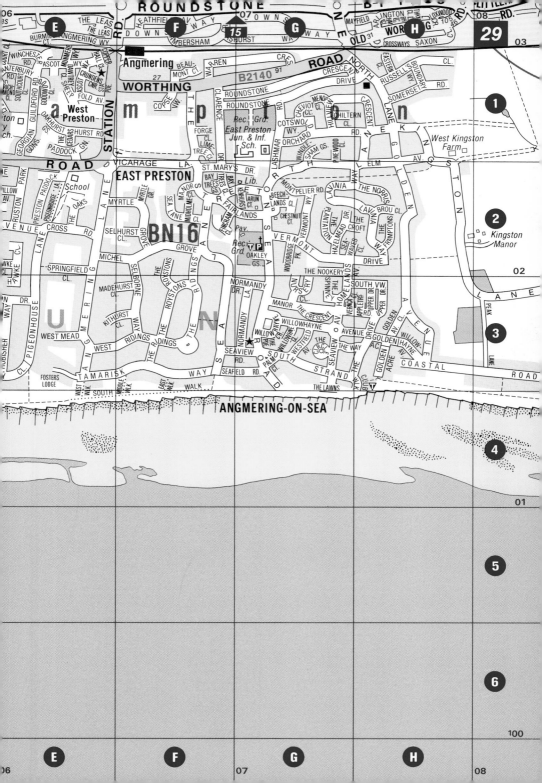

INDEX TO STREETS

HOW TO USE THIS INDEX

1. Each street name is followed by its Postal District and then by its map page reference; e.g. Abbotswood Wlk. BN16-3C 28 is in the Brighton 16 Postal District and it is to be found in square 3C on page 28. However, with the now general usage of Postal Coding, it is not recommended that this index be used as a means of addressing mail.

2. A strict alphabetical order is followed in which Av., Rd., St. etc. (even though abbreviated) are read in full and as part of the street name; e.g. Ashleigh Clo. appears after Ash La. but before Ashmere Gdns.

3. Street and Subsidiary names not shown on the Maps, appear in the Index in *Italics* with the thoroughfare to which it is connected shown in brackets; e.g. *Arcade, The. BN17-2F 27 (off Arcade Rd.)*

GENERAL ABBREVIATIONS

All : Alley	Clo : Close	Ind : Industrial	Pl : Place
App : Approach	Comn : Common	Junct : Junction	Rd : Road
Arc : Arcade	Cotts : Cottages	La : Lane	S : South
Av : Avenue	Ct : Court	Lit : Little	Sq : Square
Bk : Back	Cres : Crescent	Lwr : Lower	Sta : Station
Boulevd : Boulevard	Dri : Drive	Mnr : Manor	St : Street
Bri : Bridge	E : East	Mans : Mansions	Ter : Terrace
B'way : Broadway	Embkmt : Embankment	Mkt : Market	Up : Upper
Bldgs : Buildings	Est : Estate	M : Mews	Vs : Villas
Bus : Business	Gdns : Gardens	Mt : Mount	Wlk : Walk
Cen : Centre	Ga : Gate	N : North	W : West
Chu : Church	Gt : Great	Pal : Palace	Yd : Yard
Chyd : Churchyard	Grn : Green	Pde : Parade	
Circ : Circle	Gro : Grove	Pk : Park	
Cir : Circus	Ho : House	Pas : Passage	

INDEX TO STREETS

Abbotswood Wlk. BN16-3C 28
Abbottsbury. PO21-4C 20
A'Becket's Av. PO21-4D 20
Aberdare Clo. PO19-1F 7
Acorn Clo. BN16-5F 15
Acorn Clo. PO20-3C 18
Acorn End. PO21-3F 21
Acre Clo. BN16-1B 28
Acre St. PO20-1E 17
Addison Way. PO22-1C 22
Adelaide Rd. PO19-2F 7
Admirals Wlk. BN17-1A 28
Admiralty Gdns. PO22-5H 23
Admiralty Rd. PO22-4G 23
Aigburth Av. PO21-2F 21
Ajax Pl. PO22-4B 24
Albert Rd. BN16-1C 28
Albert Rd. BN17-2F 27
Albert Rd. PO19-3A 6
Albert Rd. PO21-5E 23
Albion Rd. PO20-5E 19
Alborough Way. PO21-3F 21
Alder Way. PO22-3D 24
Aldingbourne Caravan Pk. PO20-4A 8
Aldwick Av. PO21-6A 22
Aldwick Clo. BN16-4B 28
Aldwick Felds. PO21-2G 21
Aldwick Gdns. PO21-5A 22
Aldwick Pl. PO21-6A 22
Aldwick Rd. PO21-3G 21
Aldwick St. PO21-3G 21
Alexander Clo. PO21-3G 21
Alexandra Rd. PO19-2F 7
Alfriston Clo. PO22-3B 24
Allandale Clo. PO20-3E 19
Allangate Dri. BN16-1D 28
Alleyne Way. PO22-4G 25
Alperton Clo. PO23-2E 21
Amberley Clo. BN17-1G 27
Amberley Dri. PO21-4A 22
Amberley Rd. BN16-3C 28
Ambersham Cres. BN16-6F 15
Ambleside Clo. PO22-3A 24
Anchor Springs. BN17-2F 27
Ancton Clo. PO22-3E 25
Ancton Dri. PO22-3E 25
Ancton La. PO22-3E 25
Ancton La. Caravan Site. PO22-3F 25
Ancton Lodge La. PO22-4F 25
Ancton Way. PO22-4F 25
Andrew Av. PO22-4B 24
Andrew Clo. BN16-1B 28

Angmering La. BN16-3E 29
Angmering Way. BN16-6E 15
Annandale Av. PO21-4D 22
Anne Howard Gdns. BN18-4C 10
Anson Rd. PO21-3D 20
Apple Gro. PO21-4D 20
Appletree Rd. PO22-3E 9
Appletrees. BN16-3H 29
Apuldram La. N. PO19-3A 6
Apuldram La. S. PO20-6A 6
Arcade Rd. BN17-2F 27
Arcade, The. BN17-2F 27
(off Arcade Rd.)
Arcade, The. PO21-5E 23
Argyle Cir. PO21-5D 22
(off Argyle Rd.)
Argyle Rd. PO21-5D 22
Arlington Ter. BN16-6H 15
Armada Ct. PO20-6G 17
Armadale Rd. PO19-2F 7
Armada Way. BN17-1A 28
Arndale Rd. BN17-1D 26
Arnell Av. PO20-4E 19
Arnhem Rd. PO21-3C 22
Arnold Way. PO18-2C 4
Artex Av. BN16-6C 14
Arun Bus. Pk. PO22-3F 23
Arun Clo. BN16-1C 28
Arun Ct. BN16-2G 29
Arundel Gdns. BN17-2C 28
Arundel Rd. BN16-4F 15
Arundel Rd. BN17-2F 27
Arundel Way. PO22-4G 25
Arun Pde. BN17-3F 27
Arun Rd. PO21-4B 22
Arun St. BN18-5D 10
Arun Ter. BN18-5C 10
Arun Way. PO21-5D 20
(in two parts)
Ascot Clo. PO20-3E 17
Ascot Way. BN16-1E 29
Ashburnham Clo. PO19-2B 6
Ashcroft Way. PO21-5C 20
Ashdown Clo. BN16-5F 15
Ash Gro. PO22-1D 22
Ash Gro. Ind. Pk. PO22-1E 23
Ash La. BN16-2C 28
Ashleigh Clo. BN16-3G 15
Ashmere Gdns. PO22-4C 24
Ashmere La. PO22-4C 24
Ashton Gdns. BN16-3C 28
Ashurst Clo. PO21-2B 22
Ashurst Way. BN16-6F 15

Ashwood Dri. BN16-2C 28
Aspen Way. PO22-3D 24
Astra Clo. PO18-4C 4
Avenals, The. BN16-4G 15
Avenue App. PO19-2D 6
Avenue de Chartres. PO19-3D 6
Avenue, The. PO19-5E 3
Avenue, The. PO21-5C 22
Avisford Pk. Rd. BN18-1H 9
Avon Clo. PO22-4B 24
Avon Rd. BN17-2F 27

Badgers Wlk. BN16-5F 15
Baffins La. PO19-3E 7
Bailey Clo. BN17-6A 14
Bakers Arms Hill. BN18-4D 10
Bala Cres. PO22-3A 24
Baldwin Clo. PO22-3C 24
Balliol Clo. PO21-1G 21
Balmoral. PO19-3H 7
Balmoral Clo. PO21-3G 21
Banjo Rd. BN17-4G 27
Bank View Clo. PO22-4E 23
Barford Rd. PO19-4E 7
Barker Clo. PO18-2G 5
Barlow Rd. PO19-2C 6
Barn Clo. BN17-5G 13
Barnett Clo. PO20-1B 8
Barnett's Field. PO20-1A 8
Barnfield. PO22-4G 23
Barnfield Dri. PO19-1G 7
Barnham La. PO22 & BN18-4F 9
Barnham Rd. PO20 & PO22-1C 8
Barn Rise. PO22-4F 9
Barn Rd. PO20-4E 17
Barnside. PO18-2D 4
Barnsite Clo. BN16-1B 28
Barnsite Gdns. BN16-1B 28
Barn Wlk. PO20-5E 17
Barons Clo. PO20-2A 8
Barons Mead. PO21-5C 20
Barque Clo. BN17-1A 28
Barrack La. PO21-4F 21
Barton Clo. PO21-4C 20
Barton Ct. BN16-2B 28
Barton Rd. PO19-2C 6
Barton Rd. PO22-1B 22
Barton Way. PO20-5G 17
Basin Rd. PO19-4D 6
Bassett Rd. PO21-6D 22
Bayford Rd. BN17-3F 27
Bayton Ct. PO19-3F 7

Baytree Gdns. BN16-2F 29
Bay Trees Clo. BN16-2F 29
Bay Wlk. PO21-5E 21
Beach Clo. PO21-4E 21
Beach Gdns. PO20-6C 18
Beach Rd. BN17-3G 27
Beach Rd. PO20-3E 19
Beach Rd. PO21-6C 20
Beaconsfield Clo. PO22-4D 24
Beaconsfield Rd. BN17-6F 13
Beacon Way. BN17-1A 28
Beagle Dri. BN18-5H 9
Beatty Rd. PO21-4D 22
Beaufield Clo. PO20-6C 18
Beaumont Ct. BN16-1F 29
Beaumont Pk. BN17-3A 28
Beaver Clo. PO19-3H 5
Bedenscroft. PO21-5B 22
Bedford Av. PO21-2B 22
Bedford St. PO21-5E 23
Beech Av. PO19-3C 6
Beech Av. PO20-5G 17
Beech Clo. PO20-2A 8
Beechlands Clo. BN16-2G 29
Beech View. BN16-3G 15
(in two parts)
Beeding Clo. PO22-1F 23
Belemede Clo. PO20-4A 8
Belgrave Cres. PO19-6D 6
Bell Clo. PO19-1D 6
Bell Ct. PO21-3E 21
Bell Davies Rd. BN17-1H 27
Bell La. PO20-2H 17
Belloc Rd. BN17-6E 13
Bellscroft Clo. BN17-1H 27
Belmont St. PO21-6E 23
Belmont Ter. BN18-6G 9
Belyngham Cres. BN17-1E 27
Bennetts Clo. PO20-4E 17
Ben Turner Ind. Est. PO19-3H 7
Bereweeke Rd. PO22-4H 23
Berghestede Rd. PO22-2D 22
Bermuda Dri. BN17-1A 28
Bernard Rd. BN18-5B 10
Berri Ct. BN18-5F 9
Berrybarn La. PO20-3A 16
Berry La. BN17-3H 27
Berry La. PO22-1B 22
Berry Mill Clo. PO21-4E 23
Bersted Grn. Ct. PO22-2D 22
Bersted M. PO22-3E 23
Bersted St. PO22-3D 22
(in two parts)

Bethwines Clo. PO18-2G 5
Beverley Clo. BN18-5G 9
Beverley Clo. PO20-4E 19
Beverley Gdns. BN16-1B 28
Bewley Rd. BN16-3F 15
Bickleys Ct. PO21-6C 22
Bignor Clo. BN16-1D 28
Bilsham Ct. BN18-6F 9
Bilsham La. BN16-1C 24
Bilsham Rd. BN18-1E 25
(Bilsham)
Bilsham Rd. BN18-6F 9
(Yapton)
Binstead Av. PO22-3H 23
Binsted Clo. BN16-3B 28
Binsted La. BN18-5A 10
Birch Clo. BN16-5F 15
Birch Clo. BN18-6A 10
(Arundel)
Birch Clo. BN18-1G 9
(Walberton)
Birch Clo. PO21-2F 21
Birches Clo. PO20-4B 18
Birdham Clo. PO21-3A 22
Birdham Rd. PO19-6B 6
Biscay Clo. BN17-1B 28
Bishop Luffa Clo. PO19-2B 6
Bishops Clo. PO21-5C 20
Bishopsgate Wlk. PO19-2F 7
Blackboy La. PO18-3G 5
Black Horse Caravan Pk. PO20-3B 18
(off Mill La.)
Blakehurst La. BN18-5H 11
Blakehurst Way. BN17-1F 27
Blakemyle. PO21-6A 22
Blakes Rd. PO22-4H 23
Blanford Rd. PO19-1F 7
Blenheim Ct. PO21-1G 21
Blenheim Gdns. PO19-3G 7
Blenheim Rd. BN18-6F 9
Blondell Dri. PO21-3F 21
Bluecedars Clo. BN16-6E 15
Bognor Rd. PO19 & PO20-3G 7
Boleyn Dri. PO21-4D 20
Bond St. BN18-4C 10
Bonnar Clo. PO20-5B 18
Bonnar Rd. PO20-5C 18
Bookers La. PO20-3H 17
Bosham La. PO18-4B 4
Botany Clo. BN16-3D 28
Boundary Way. BN16-1H 29
Bourne Clo. PO19-2G 5
Bourne Ct. PO20-6F 17
Bowley La. PO20-1B 20
Bowling Grn. Clo. PO21-4D 20
Boxgrove Gdns. PO21-3E 21
Box Tree Av. BN16-2B 28
Bracklesham Bay Caravan & Boat Club.
                              PO20-6H 17
Bracklesham Clo. PO20-5G 17
Bracklesham La. PO20-5G 17
Bradlond Clo. PO21-6B 22
Bradshaw Rd. PO19-1G 7
Braemar Way. PO21-1A 22
Bramber Clo. PO21-4B 22
Bramber Rd. PO19-4F 7
Bramber Sq. BN16-1C 28
Brambletyne Clo. BN16-3G 15
Bramblings, The. BN16-2D 28
Bramfield Rd. PO22-5B 24
Bramley Gdns. PO22-1C 22
Brampton Clo. PO20-4C 18
Brandyhole La. PO19-5C 2
Brazwick Av. PO21-1A 22
Bread La. BN17-3A 26
Bream La. PO20-3A 18
Brendon Way. BN16-1B 28
Brent Rd. PO21-4B 22
Brewery Hill. BN18-4D 10
Briar Av. PO20-2E 17
Briar Clo. BN16-5F 15
Briar Clo. BN18-5F 9
Briar Cottage Caravan Pk. PO20-2F 17
Brideoake Clo. PO19-1C 6
Bridge Rd. BN17-2C 28
Bridge Rd. PO19-2F 7
Bridgeway, The. PO20-5C 18
Bridle Way, The. PO20-4C 18
Bridorley Clo. PO21-3D 20
Brigham Pl. PO22-5C 24
Bristol Gdns. PO19-5D 2

Broadbridge Dri. PO18-2C 4
Broadbridge Mill. PO18-2C 4
Broadmark Av. BN16-3C 28
Broadmark La. BN16-3C 28
Broadmark Pde. BN17-2C 28
Broadmark Way. BN16-3C 28
Broad Strand. BN16-3C 28
Broad View. PO20-4E 19
Broadway. PO20-3B 6
Broadway, The. PO19-5E 3
Bronze Clo. PO22-1D 22
Brook Av. PO18-4B 4
Brook Clo. PO21-4B 22
Brookenbee Clo. BN16-6B 14
Brooklands. PO21-4C 20
Brook La. PO22-6E 9
Brookpit La. BN17-3A 26
(in two parts)
Brookside Av. BN16-6C 14
Brookside Caravan Site. BN17-4E 13
Brooks La. PO18-2D 4
(in two parts)
Brooks La. PO22-3F 23
Brooks La. W. PO22-3E 23
Brooksmead. PO22-4F 23
Broomcroft Rd. PO22-5B 24
Broomfield Rd. PO20-3E 19
Brou Clo. BN16-2H 29
Broyle Clo. PO19-6D 2
Broyle Rd. PO19-6D 2
Brunswick Clo. PO22-3H 23
Buckingham Dri. PO19-3H 7
Buckland Dri. PO21-3D 20
Bucknor Clo. PO21-3E 21
Bucksham Av. PO21-1A 22
Burchett Wlk. PO21-3A 22
Burley Rd. PO22-5C 24
Burlington Gdns. PO20-5E 19
Burmill Ct. BN16-6E 15
Burndell Rd. BN18-5G 9
Burngreave Ct. PO21-5C 22
Burnham Av. PO21-5D 22
Burnham Gdns. PO21-5D 22
Burnhill Ct. BN16-6E 15
Burns Gdns. PO22-3C 24
Bursledon Clo. PO22-3H 23
Burwash Clo. BN16-6H 15
Bushby Av. BN16-2C 28
Buttermere Way. BN17-1A 28
Byeway, The. PO20-2B 16
Bye Way, The. PO21-5E 21
Byfield Pl. PO22-2E 23
Byron Clo. PO22-3C 24
Byron Rd. BN17-6A 26
Bywater Way. PO19-5D 6
Byways. PO20-2B 16
Byway, The. PO22-4D 24

Caernarvon Rd. PO19-3H 7
Cakeham Rd. PO20-2A 16
Cakeham Way. PO20-4D 16
Calceto La. BN17-1F 13
Caledon Av. PO22-4C 24
Caledonian Rd. PO19-3E 7
California M. BN18-5C 10
Cambrai Av. PO19-4F 7
Cambria Clo. PO18-4C 4
Cambridge Av. PO20-3D 16
Cambridge Dri. PO21-4A 22
Cambridge Wlk. PO21-4A 22
Campbell Dri. BN16-1B 28
Campbell Rd. PO21-5E 23
Canada Gro. PO21-5D 22
Canada Rd. BN18-4B 10
Canal Rd. BN18-6F 9
Canal Wharf. PO19-4D 6
Canning Rd. PO22-5G 23
Canon La. PO19-3D 6
Canon's Clo. PO21-4F 21
Canterbury Clo. PO19-1D 6
Canterbury Rd. PO21-4C 20
Canterbury Rd. BN16-1E 29
Canute Rd. PO18-4B 4
Cape, The. BN17-2A 28
Capstan Dri. BN17-1A 28
Caravan Clo, The. BN17-6G 13
Cardinals Dri. PO21-4C 20
Carleton Rd. PO19-1C 6
Carlingford Ct. PO21-4D 22
Carlisle Gdns. PO19-6D 2

Carlton Av. PO21-2E 21
Carousel Ct. PO22-3C 22
Carvel Way. BN17-1A 28
Cassells Rd. PO19-5D 2
(in two parts)
Castle Gdns. BN18-4C 10
Castleman Rd. PO19-1G 7
Castlereagh Grn. PO22-3H 23
Cathedral Way. PO19-3B 6
Causeway, The. BN18-6E 11
Causeway, The. PO20-3B 18
Causeway, The. PO21-5C 20
Cavendish Rd. PO21-5D 22
Cavendish St. PO19-2D 6
Cawley Rd. PO19-4E 7
Cedar Clo. PO21-2F 21
Cedar Clo. E. PO21-2G 21
Cedar Dri. PO19-3C 6
Cedars, The. BN16-1E 29
Central Av. BN16-3C 28
Central Av. PO21-2B 22
Central Dri. PO21-2A 22
Central Dri. PO22-4F 25
Ceres Pl. PO22-5C 24
Chainbridge La. PO20-2A 18
Chalcraft La. PO21-1G 21
Chalfont Clo. PO22-4D 24
Chalkpit La. PO18-1F 3
Chanctonbury Rd. BN16-3B 28
Chandler Rd. PO19-4C 6
Channel Keep. BN17-3G 27
Channel View. PO21-5C 20
Chantryfield Rd. BN16-3F 15
Chapel Clo. BN17-1E 27
Chapel La. PO20-1E 17
Chapel St. PO19-2D 6
Chapel St. PO21-5D 22
Chapel Wlk. BN16-4F 15
Charles Av. PO19-3H 7
Charlmead. PO20-5E 17
Charlwood St. PO21-6C 22
Charnwood Rd. PO22-2C 22
Chatfield Rd. PO19-1G 7
Chatsworth Dri. BN16-6B 14
Chatsworth Rd. PO19-3H 7
Chaucer Av. BN16-2B 28
Chaucer Way. PO22-3C 24
Chawkmare Coppice. PO21-3G 21
Chayle Gdns. PO20-5D 18
Cheam Rd. BN16-3D 28
Chequer La. PO18-3D 4
Cherry Av. BN18-6F 9
Cherry Clo. PO21-3F 21
Cherry Croft. BN16-6F 13
Cherry Gdns. PO20-6C 18
Cherry Orchard Rd. PO19-4F 7
Cherry Tree Dri. PO20-1C 8
Chesswood Av. PO22-3B 24
Chestnut Av. PO19-4D 2
Chestnut Clo. BN16-5F 15
Chestnut Clo. BN16-2G 29
Chestnut Gro. PO22-2D 22
Cheveley Gdns. PO21-3F 21
Cheviot St. BN16-1G 29
Chichester Airfield. PO18-4G 3
Chichester By-Pass. PO18 & PO19-1E 5
Chichester Ct. BN16-2C 28
Chichester Rd. BN18-4A 10
Chichester Rd. PO20-3D 18
Chichester Way. PO20-3F 19
Chilgrove Pl. BN18-6G 9
Chiltern Clo. BN16-1G 29
Chine, The. BN17-3A 28
Chipley Ct. PO21-4B 22
Christchurch Cres. PO21-2G 21
Christie Pl. PO22-2E 23
Church App. BN17-2G 27
Church Clo. PO21-6A 20
Church Farm Holiday Village. PO21
                              -6A 20
Church Farm La. PO20-3F 17
Churchill Av. PO21-1G 21
Churchill Pde. BN17-2C 28
(off Street, The)
Churchill Wlk. PO21-5C 20
(off Ashcroft Way)
Church La. BN17-2A 26
(Climping)
Church La. BN17-3E 13
(Lyminster)
Church La. PO20-2B 8

Church La. PO21-5A 20
Church La. PO22-5E 9
(Barnham)
Church La. PO22-3D 22
(South Bersted)
Churchmead Clo. PO18-1D 2
Church Meadow. PO18-4B 4
Church Path. PO21-4E 23
Church Path. PO22-4E 25
Church Rd. BN16-4F 15
(Angmering)
Church Rd. BN16-2C 28
(Rustington)
Church Rd. BN18-5F 9
Church Rd. PO19-2G 7
Church Rd. PO20-4E 17
(East Wittering)
Church Rd. PO20-3D 18
(Selsey)
Churchside. PO19-2D 6
Church St. BN17-2G 27
Church Way. PO21-4C 20
Cinders La. BN18-6G 9
Circle, The. BN16-3G 29
City Bus. Cen. PO19-4D 6
Claigmar Rd. BN16-2C 28
Clappers La. PO20-5G 17
Clarence Av. BN17-6E 13
Clarence Dri. BN16-1F 29
Clarence Rd. PO21-5E 23
Clay La. BN18-6H 11
Clay La. PO18 & PO19-1F 5
Claypit La. PO18-3H 3
Clayton La. PO20-4G 17
Clayton Rd. PO20-5B 18
Cleveland Rd. PO19-4F 7
Clevetts, The. PO21-4E 21
Clifton Rd. BN17-3F 27
Clifton Rd. PO21-4D 22
Climping St. BN17-3A 26
Clock Pk. PO22-2F 23
Cloisters, The. BN17-3H 27
Close, The. BN16-3D 28
Close, The. PO19-3D 6
Close, The. PO20-3F 19
Close, The. PO21-5E 21
Close, The. PO22-4F 25
Clovelly Av. PO22-4A 24
Club Wlk. BN16-3H 29
Clun Rd. BN17-6D 12
Clyde Rd. PO22-5G 23
Clydesdale Av. PO19-4E 7
Clydesdale Gdns. PO22-1B 22
Coach Ho. Clo. PO20-4D 18
Coastal Rd. BN16-3H 29
Coastguard La. PO20-2A 16
Coastguard Pde. PO21-4F 21
(off Barrack La.)
Coastguard Rd. BN17-4F 27
Cobham Clo. BN18-6F 9
Cohen Clo. PO20-4A 8
Colebrook Rd. BN17-6E 13
College Clo. PO21-4A 22
College La. PO19-6E 3
Collyer Av. PO21-3B 22
Colt's Bay. PO21-4E 21
Colt St. PO20-3C 18
Commonmead La. PO21-2C 20
Compass Clo. BN17-1A 28
Compton Clo. PO19-4E 3
Compton Dri. PO22-3C 24
Conbar Av. BN16-1C 28
Conduit Mead. PO19-1G 7
Coney Clo. PO20-5E 17
Coney Rd. PO20-5E 17
Coney Six. PO20-5E 17
Coniston Clo. PO22-3A 24
Coniston Way. BN17-6A 14
Connaught Rd. BN17-2F 27
Constable Dri. PO20-4E 19
Conway Dri. PO21-5C 20
Coomes Way. BN17-5F 13
Cooper St. PO19-3E 7
Cootes La. PO22-4E 25
Copeland Rd. PO22-4H 23
Copper Hall Clo. BN16-1E 29
Coppice La. PO20-3C 18
Copse, The. PO19-5E 3
Copse View. BN16-1F 29
Copthorne Caravan Site. PO21-1F 21
Copthorne Way. PO21-1F 21

Corbishley Grn. PO22-2D 22
Corbishley Rd. PO22-2D 22
Cormorant Way. PO20-5F 17
Cornfield Clo. BN17-6G 13
Cornwall Gdns. BN17-1F 27
Cornwall Rd. BN17-1F 27
Cotland Rd. PO20-5E 19
Cotswold Way. BN16-1G 29
Cottage Clo. PO21-3E 21
Cottrells, The. BN16-4F 15
Council Cotts. BN18-1B 14
Countisbury Clo. PO21-5A 22
Courtlands Way. PO22-3B 24
Court, The. PO21-4C 20
Courtwick La. BN17-5D 12
(in two parts)
Courtwick Rd. BN17-6E 13
Coventry Clo. PO21-1F 21
Cove Rd. BN16-3B 28
Cowdray Dri. BN16-6B 14
Coxes Rd. PO20-5B 18
Crablands. PO20-4B 18
Crablands Clo. PO20-4C 18
Crab Tree Clo. BN17-4F 13
Craigwell La. PO21-3G 21
Craigwell Mnr. PO21-4F 21
Crane St. PO19-3E 7
Cranford Gdns. PO21-4D 22
Crede Clo. PO18-4C 4
Crede La. PO18-3C 4
Creek End. PO19-3H 5
Crescenta Wlk. PO21-5B 22
Crescent Rd. PO21-5D 22
Crescent, The. BN16-3G 29
(East Preston)
Crescent, The. BN16-2B 28
(Rustington)
Crescent, The. PO20-4D 16
Crescent, The. PO21-5C 20
Crescent, The. PO22-4H 23
Critchfield Rd. PO18-4B 4
Critchmere Dri. PO22-3C 8
Croftcost La. PO22-3C 24
Croft Mead. PO19-5E 3
Croft Rd. PO20-5C 18
Croft, The. BN16-2H 29
Croft, The. PO21-3A 22
Croft Way. PO20-4C 18
Croft Way. PO22-3B 24
Crookthorn La. BN17-3A 26
Crosbie Clo. PO19-6D 6
Crossbush By-Pass. BN18-1G 13
Crossbush Rd. PO22-5A 24
Cross Rd. BN16-2E 29
Crossways. BN16-6H 15
Crossways. PO22-3E 25
Crossways, The. BN17-6E 13
Croy Clo. PO19-5C 6
Crundens Corner. BN16-1E 29
Cudlow Av. BN16-2C 28
Cudlow Gdns. BN16-3C 28
Culmore Clo. PO20-4D 16
Culmore Rd. PO20-4D 16
Culver Rd. PO22-4H 23
Cumberland Clo. BN16-4G 15
Cumberland Cres. BN16-4F 15
Cumberland Rd. BN16-4G 15
Cunliffe Clo. PO20-1B 16
Cunningham Gdns. PO22-4B 24
Curlescroft. PO21-6A 22
Cutfield Clo. PO19-6D 6
Cygnet Wlk. PO22-2C 22
Cypress Way. PO21-4F 21

Dairy La. BN18-1G 9
Dallaway Rd. PO19-5F 7
Dalloway Rd. BN18-5A 10
Daltons Pl. BN18-5C 10
Dame School Ct. PO18-2E 3
Danefield Rd. PO20-5B 18
Dapper's La. BN16-3G 15
Dark La. PO18-2C 4
(in two parts)
Davenport Rd. PO22-4H 23
Davids Clo. PO21-3A 22
Davits Dri. BN17-1A 28
Dawtrey Clo. BN16-1E 29
Dean Clo. BN17-6E 13
Decoy Dri. BN16-2F 15
Deer Pk. La. PO20-3A 18

Deeside Av. PO19-2H 5
Defiance Pl. PO22-5B 24
Dell Dri. BN16-5F 15
Delling Clo. PO18-3B 4
Delling La. PO18-4C 4
Dell, The. PO22-2B 22
Dempsey Rd. PO19-5E 3
Den Av. PO21-5E 23
Denham Clo. PO22-4D 24
Dennys Clo. PO20-4D 18
Denshare Rd. PO20-3D 18
Densihale. PO21-5B 22
Derwent Clo. BN17-1A 28
Derwent Gro. PO22-3A 24
Devonshire Pl. PO21-5D 22
Devonshire Rd. PO21-5C 22
Dial Clo. PO22-4F 9
Dickinson Pl. PO22-2E 23
Dingley Rd. PO22-2B 28
Dinsdale Gdns. BN16-1C 28
(in three parts)
Ditchfield Clo. PO22-3C 24
Dolphin Clo. PO19-3H 5
Dolphin M. PO19-3B 6
Dolphin Way. BN16-3D 28
Dominion Way. BN16-6C 14
Donegal Rd. PO19-6E 3
Dorset Rd. PO21-3D 22
Douglas Clo. BN18-6H 9
Douglas Martin Rd. PO19-2F 7
Downing Clo. PO21-1G 21
Downlands Clo. PO21-3C 20
Downlands Ct. PO19-2D 6
Downs Way. BN16-6F 15
Downview Clo. BN18-5G 9
Downview Clo. PO18-1C 2
Downview Clo. PO20-5F 17
Downview Rd. BN18-5G 9
Downview Rd. PO22-2D 8
(Barnham)
Downview Rd. PO22-3H 23
(Felpham)
Downview Way. BN18-5G 9
Drake Cres. BN18-6H 9
Drake Pk. PO22-4B 24
Drift La. PO20-3B 18
Drift Rd. PO20-2E 19
Drift Rd. PO21-3D 20
Driftway, The. BN16-1B 28
Drive, The. BN16-3H 29
Drive, The. PO18-5C 4
Drive, The. PO19-4D 2
Drive, The. PO21-4G 21
Drove La. PO20-5H 17
Dryad Way. PO22-5C 24
Drygrounds La. PO22-3G 23
Duck La. PO20-3A 18
Dukes Clo. BN18-5B 10
Dukes Meadow. PO21-2D 20
Duke St. BN17-2F 27
Duncan Rd. PO19-1C 6
Duncton Clo. PO22-5A 24
Duncton Rd. BN16-6C 14
Dunes, The. PO21-5E 21
Dunstan Clo. PO19-4E 3
Durban Pk. PO22-3E 23
Durban Rd. PO22-2D 22
Durham Clo. PO21-5C 20
Durham Gdns. PO19-6D 2
Durlston Dri. PO22-2C 22
Durnford Clo. PO19-2C 6

Eagles Clo. BN17-5E 13
Earnley Rd. PO20-4H 17
East Av. PO22-3E 25
E. Bank. PO20-4E 19
E. Bank Way. BN17-3A 28
(off Ketch Rd.)
E. Beach Rd. PO20-3F 19
E. Bracklesham Dri. PO20-6G 17
E. Bracklesham Dri. Caravan Pk. PO20
-6H 17
East Clo. PO22-4D 24
Eastcourt Way. BN16-1E 29
East Dri. BN16-6E 15
East Dri. PO22-4F 25
Eastergate Grn. BN16-2C 28
Easter Ga. Ho. PO20-2B 8
Eastergate La. PO20 & BN18-1C 8
Eastern Clo. BN16-1H 29

E. Front Rd. PO21-6C 20
Eastgate Sq. PO19-3E 7
East Ham Rd. BN17-2E 27
E. Lake. PO21-4E 23
Eastland Rd. PO19-5F 7
E. Mead. PO21-5C 20
Eastover Way. PO22-4G 23
E. Pallant. PO19-3E 7
East Row. PO19-3E 7
East St. BN17-2F 27
East St. PO19-3E 7
East St. PO20-4C 18
East Wlk. BN16-3F 29
E. Walls. PO19-3E 7
E. Walls Clo. PO19-3E 7
East Way. PO20-4E 19
E. Wittering Bus. Cen. PO20-3F 17
Edinburgh Clo. PO21-3G 21
Edwen Clo. PO21-2D 20
Eels Cross. PO20-3A 18
Elbridge Cres. PO21-3E 21
Eldon Way. BN17-1D 26
Eleanor Gdns. PO22-4C 24
Elfin Gro. PO21-5C 22
Elfin M. PO21-5C 22
Elizabeth Av. PO21-1E 21
Elizabeth Clo. PO21-2H 21
Elizabeth Rd. PO19-2H 7
Ella Clo. PO20-4D 16
Ella Nore La. PO20-1A 16
Ellasdale Rd. PO21-5C 22
Ella Ter. BN18-1C 14
Ellis Clo. BN18-5B 10
Ellis Way. PO21-5C 20
Elm Clo. PO20-5G 17
Elm Clo. PO21-4C 20
Elmcroft Pl. PO20-3A 8
Elm Dri. PO22-4G 25
Elmer Clo. PO22-4G 25
Elmer Ct. PO22-4H 25
Elmer Rd. PO22-4D 24
Elm Gro. PO20-4C 18
Elm Gro. PO21-5B 22
Elm Gro. PO22-2D 8
Elmgrove Rd. BN17-1G 27
Elm Gro. S. PO22-3D 8
Elmhurst Clo. BN16-3G 15
Elm Pk. PO18-3C 4
Elm Pl. BN16-1D 28
Elm Rd. PO20-2A 8
Elms Field. PO20-4C 18
Elms La. PO20-2B 16
Elms Rise. PO20-2B 16
Elmstead Gdns. PO20-1B 16
Elmstead Pk. Rd. PO20-1B 16
Elms Way. PO20-1B 16
Elm Tree Clo. PO20-3D 18
Elmwood Av. PO22-3E 23
Elspring Mead. BN17-6E 13
Ely Gdns. PO21-2F 21
Ensign Way. BN17-1A 28
Esher Clo. PO21-3D 20
Esher Dri. BN17-2H 27
Esmonde Clo. BN17-1H 27
Esplanade, The. PO21-6E 23
Esplanade, The. PO22-5G 23
Essex Rd. PO21-3D 22
Estuary, The. BN17-2H 27
Eton Clo. PO21-1G 21
Eton Dri. PO20-3E 17
Ettrick Clo. PO19-4F 7
Ettrick Rd. PO19-4E 7
Evans Pl. PO22-2E 23
Evelyn Av. BN16-3D 28
Ewens Gdns. PO22-2D 8
Exeter Clo. PO21-5A 22
Exeter Rd. PO19-6C 2
Exton Rd. PO19-5F 7

Fairfield Clo. PO18-4C 4
Fairfield Rd. PO18-4B 4
Fairholme Dri. BN18-6G 9
Fairlands. BN16-2F 29
Fairlands. PO22-2B 22
Fairlawn. BN16-1C 28
Fairlead. BN17-3H 27
Fairway. BN17-3H 27
Fairway, The. PO21-5D 20
Falcon Gdns. BN17-5E 13
Falkland Av. BN17-1H 27

Falklands Clo. PO22-3E 23
Faresmead. PO21-6A 22
Farm Clo. PO22-4G 25
Farm Corner. PO22-4F 25
Farm Rd. PO20-6G 17
Farm Way. BN16-2B 28
Farndell Clo. PO19-2G 7
Farnhurst Rd. PO22-3E 9
Faroes, The. BN17-6A 14
Fastnet Way. BN17-1A 28
Fatting Ground La. PO22-6D 8
Felpham Gdns. PO22-4A 24
Felpham Rd. PO22-5G 23
Felpham Way. PO22-4F 23
Ferndale Rd. PO19-5E 3
Ferndale Wlk. BN16-3G 15
Ferndown Gdns. PO22-3H 23
Fernhurst Gdns. PO21-3F 21
Ferring Gdns. PO22-3H 23
Ferry Rd. BN17-3C 26
Festival Ct. PO19-2D 6
Field Clo. BN18-1G 9
Field Pl. BN17-2F 27
Field Rd. PO20-4F 17
Fincham Clo. BN16-2F 29
Finch Clo. BN17-5E 13
Finch Gdns. PO22-1C 22
Findon Dri. PO22-3C 24
Finisterre Way. BN17-3A 28
Fircroft Cres. BN16-1D 28
Firs Av. PO22-4A 24
Firs Av. W. PO22-4A 24
First Av. PO20-6G 17
First Av. PO22-5A 24
(Felpham)
First Av. PO22-3E 25
(Middleton-on-Sea)
Fishbourne Rd. E. PO19-3A 6
Fishbourne Rd. W. PO19-3H 5
Fishermans Wlk. PO20-4E 19
Fishermans Wlk. PO21-4F 21
Fish La. PO20-3A 18
Fish La. PO21-6A 22
Fittleworth Dri. PO22-3B 24
Fittleworth Gdns. BN16-2C 28
Fitzalan Rd. BN17-3G 27
Fitzalan Rd. BN18-6C 10
Fitzwilliam Clo. PO21-4A 22
Flansham La. PO22-4B 24
Flansham Pk. PO22-3B 24
Flaxman Av. PO19-3B 6
Flax Mean. PO22-4A 24
Flax Mean Ho. PO22-4A 24
Fleet Clo. BN17-1A 28
Fletcher Clo. PO21-3D 20
Fletcher Way. BN16-3F 15
Florence Rd. PO19-3G 7
Follett Clo. PO21-4G 21
Fontwell Av. PO20-1B 8
Fontwell Clo. BN16-3B 28
Fontwell Rd. PO20-3F 19
Ford Airfield Ind. Est. BN18-5H 9
Ford Ho. Caravan Pk. BN18-4A 12
Ford La. BN18-5A 12
Ford Rd. BN17-1E 27
Ford Rd. BN18-6A 12
Ford Rd. Ind. Est. BN17-1D 26
Fordwater Gdns. BN18-6H 9
Fordwater La. PO19-5E 3
Fordwater Rd. PO18-2E 3
(in two parts)
Fordwater Rd. PO19-5E 3
Forge Clo. BN16-1F 29
Forge Clo. PO19-6C 6
Fosters Lodge. BN16-3E 29
Foundry Rd. BN18-6F 9
Fourth Av. PO22-5B 24
Foxdale Dri. BN16-5F 15
Foxes Croft. PO22-3F 9
Foxwarren Clo. PO20-4E 17
Framptons, The. BN16-2H 29
Franciscan Way. BN17-2F 27
Frandor Rd. PO21-3A 22
Franklin Pl. PO19-2E 7
Fraser Clo. PO20-5E 19
Frederick Rd. PO19-3A 6
Freeways. PO20-3B 18
Friary Clo. PO22-4D 24
Friary La. PO19-3E 7
Frith Rd. PO21-4B 22
Frobisher Rd. PO21-3E 21

Frobisher Way. BN16-3E 29
Furse Feld. PO21-6B 22
Furzedown. BN17-3G 27
Furzefield. PO20-2E 17
Furzefield Clo. BN16-2F 15

Gainsboro Rd. PO21-5D 22
Gainsborough Dri. PO20-4D 18
Garden Av. PO20-5G 17
Garden Clo. BN16-3G 15
Garden Cottage. PO18-4B 4
Garden Ct. PO21-3G 21
Garland Clo. PO19-4F 7
Genoa Clo. BN17-1A 28
George IV Wlk. PO22-3H 23
Georgian Gdns. BN16-1E 29
Gifford Rd. PO18-2C 4
Gilbert Rd. PO19-1C 6
Gilberts, The. BN16-4B 28
Giles Clo. BN18-6F 9
Gillway. PO20-3F 19
Gilmore Rd. PO19-3G 7
Gilpin Clo. BN19-3H 5
Gilwynes. PO21-6A 22
Gilwynes Ct. PO21-6A 22
Glade, The. PO21-5C 20
Gladstone Rd. BN18-6F 9
Gladstone Ter. BN17-5F 13
Glamis Ct. PO21-5E 23
Glamis St. PO21-5E 23
Glandonian Rd. BN17-6F 13
Glencathara Rd. PO21-5C 22
Glen Cres. PO20-4D 18
Glenelg Clo. PO21-2A 22
Glenville Rd. BN16-3C 28
Glenway. PO22-4E 23
Glenwood Av. PO22-4E 23
Globe Pl. BN17-6F 13
Gloster Dri. PO21-4D 20
Gloucester La. BN17-2F 27
Gloucester Pl. BN17-2F 27
Gloucester Rd. BN17-2E 27
Gloucester Rd. PO21-5F 23
Gloucester Way. PO19-6D 2
Glynde Cres. PO22-3H 23
Goatlands Caravan Pk. PO20-3B 18
Goda Rd. BN17-2G 27
Godman Clo. PO21-2F 21
Godwin Way. PO18-1G 5
Goldcrest Av. BN17-5E 13
Golden Acre. BN16-3H 29
Golden Acre. PO21-5C 20
Golden Clo. BN16-1H 29
Golf Links La. PO20-1B 18
Golf Links Rd. PO22-2G 23
  (in two parts)
Goodacres. PO22-4F 9
Goodhew Clo. BN18-5G 9
Goodwood Av. PO22-3G 23
Goodwood Clo. BN16-1E 29
Goodwood Motor Circuit. PO18-4G 3
Gordon Av. PO19-6C 6
Gordon Av. PO22-4E 23
  (in two parts)
Gordon Av. W. PO22-3E 23
Gordon Ter. BN18-1C 14
Gorse Av. PO22-3C 24
Gosden Rd. BN17-1H 27
Gospond Rd. PO22-4E 9
Gossamer La. PO21-2F 21
Graffham Clo. PO19-4E 3
Grafton Av. PO22-3B 24
Grafton Clo. BN16-1C 28
Grafton Rd. PO20-6D 18
  (in two parts)
Graham Rd. BN18-6F 9
Granary Way. BN17-5F 13
Grand Av. BN17-6E 13
Grange Ct. PO21-4G 21
Grange Field Way. PO21-3F 21
Grange La. PO21-1F 19
Grangeway, The. BN16-2C 28
Grangewood Dri. PO21-3F 21
Grant Clo. PO20-4C 18
Granville Rd. BN17-3G 27
Grassmere Clo. PO22-4G 23
Gravel La. PO19-4G 7
Gravits La. PO18-4B 22
Graydon Av. PO19-5C 6
Graylingwell Cotts. PO19-5E 3

Grayswood Av. PO20-5G 17
Greenacres Ring. BN16-3G 15
Greenbushes Clo. BN16-3B 28
Greencourt Dri. PO21-3B 22
Greenfield Rd. PO19-2G 7
Greenfields. BN17-6D 12
Green La. PO18-3C 4
  (Bosham)
Green La. PO18-1A 4
  (Broadbridge)
Green La. PO19-2F 7
Green La. PO20-5C 18
  (Selsey)
Green La. Clo. BN18-5B 10
Green Lawns Caravan Pk. PO20-3C 18
Greenlea Av. PO21-3D 20
Green, The. PO21-5C 20
Green Way. PO22-4E 25
Greenways. PO21-4D 20
Greenwood Av. PO22-2C 22
Greenwood Clo. PO22-2C 22
Greenwood Dri. BN16-5F 15
Grevatt's La. BN18-2E 25
  (in two parts)
Grevatt's La. W. BN18-1E 25
Greyfriars Clo. PO21-5A 22
Greynville Clo. PO21-3E 21
Greystone Av. PO21-1A 22
Griffin Cres. BN17-5F 13
Grosvenor Gdns. PO21-2E 21
Grosvenor Rd. PO19-5D 6
Grosvenor Way. PO21-2E 21
Grove Cres. BN17-1G 27
Grove Pk. PO19-3B 6
Grove Rd. PO19-4F 7
Grove Rd. PO20-5D 18
Grove, The. PO22-4H 23
Guernsey Farm La. PO22-4B 24
Guilden Rd. PO19-3F 7
Guildford Pl. PO19-6D 2
Guildford Rd. BN16-1E 29
Guildhall St. PO19-2E 7
Gunwin Clo. PO21-3F 21

Hacketts Rew. PO19-3E 3
Hadley Clo. PO22-3D 24
Hailsham Clo. BN16-6H 15
Hales Footpath. PO22-3H 23
Halfrey Clo. PO18-2G 5
Halfrey Rd. PO18-2G 5
Halliford Dri. PO22-3F 9
Halliwick Gdns. PO22-5A 24
Halnaker Gdns. PO21-3E 21
Hambledon Pl. PO21-5C 22
Hamilton Gdns. PO21-3F 21
Ham Mnr. Clo. BN16-5E 15
Ham Mnr. Way. BN16-5E 15
Hampden Clo. PO22-4E 25
Hampshire Av. PO21-3C 22
Hampton Ct. PO21-4A 22
Hampton Fields. BN17-1F 27
Hannah Sq. PO19-2B 6
Hanover Clo. PO20-4E 19
Harberton Cres. PO19-4D 2
Harbour Ct. PO18-4C 4
Harbour Rd. PO18-5B 4
Harbour Rd. PO21-6B 20
Harbour View Rd. PO21-4C 20
Harbour Way. PO18-5C 4
Harcourt Way. PO20-3E 19
Hardham Clo. BN16-3B 28
Hardham Rd. PO19-4F 7
Hard, The. PO22-4H 25
Hardy Clo. PO22-4C 24
Harefield Gdns. PO22-4E 25
Harefield Rd. PO22-4E 25
Hare La. PO20-3A 18
Haresfold Rd. BN16-4B 28
Harmony Dri. PO20-6G 17
Harrow Dri. PO20-3E 17
Harsfold Clo. BN16-3B 28
Harting Rd. BN17-6F 13
Hartings, The. PO22-3C 24
Harwood Ind. Est. BN17-1E 27
Harwood Rd. BN17-1E 27
Hastings Clo. PO21-4A 22
Hatherleigh Rd. PO21-3B 22
Hatherleigh Gdns. PO21-3B 22
Havelock Clo. PO22-5G 23
Havelock Rd. PO21-4D 22

Havenstoke Clo. PO19-6E 3
Haven, The. BN17-2A 28
  (in two parts)
Hawke Clo. BN16-2E 29
Hawkins Clo. PO21-3D 20
Hawks Pl. PO22-2C 22
Hawley Rd. BN16-3B 28
Hawthorn Clo. BN16-3C 28
Hawthorn Clo. PO19-2D 6
Hawthorn Rd. BN17-5E 13
Hawthorn Rd. PO21-5B 22
Haydon Clo. PO21-4E 21
Hayley's Gdns. PO22-4H 23
Hay Rd. PO19-5F 7
Haywards Clo. PO22-3H 23
Hazel Gro. BN18-5A 10
Hazel Gro. PO21-2F 21
Hazelmead Dri. BN16-2G 29
Hazel Rd. PO22-2C 22
Hearn Field Rd. BN17-5F 13
Heather Ct. PO19-4D 6
Heathfield Av. BN16-6F 15
Heath Pl. PO22-1E 23
Hechle Wood. PO21-6A 22
Hedge End. PO22-3F 9
Hedgeway. PO22-4C 24
Heghbrok Way. PO21-6B 22
Helyer's Grn. BN17-1E 27
Hendon Av. BN16-4A 28
Henfield Way. PO22-3C 24
Henry Av. BN16-2A 28
Henry Clo. PO19-3H 7
Henry St. PO21-4E 23
Henty Clo. BN18-1H 9
Henty Gdns. PO19-3C 6
Heo Grn. BN17-6D 12
Herald Dri. PO19-4E 7
Hercules Pl. PO22-4C 24
Hereford Clo. PO19-6D 2
Heritage, The. PO19-3F 7
Herne Gdns. BN16-1D 28
Herne La. BN16-1D 28
Heron Clo. PO20-3A 18
Heron Clo. PO22-1C 22
Heron Ct. BN16-3C 28
Heron Ct. PO19-2H 7
Heron Mead. PO21-6B 20
Herrington Rd. BN18-5B 10
Hersee Way. PO20-4B 18
Hertford Clo. PO21-5A 22
Heston Gro. PO21-4E 21
Hewarts La. PO21-2F 21
Hide Gdns. BN16-1B 28
Highcroft Av. PO22-3E 23
Highcroft Clo. PO22-3F 23
Highcroft Cres. PO22-3F 23
Highdown Dri. BN17-6G 13
Highfield. BN17-6D 12
Highfield Clo. BN16-4G 15
Highfield Gdns. BN16-2B 28
Highfield Gdns. PO22-3E 23
Highfield Rd. PO22-3E 23
Highgate Dri. PO21-1A 22
Highground La. PO22-5D 8
Highland Av. PO21-4C 22
Highland Rd. PO19-5D 2
High Ridge La. BN18-6B 10
High St. Angmering, BN16-4F 15
High St. Arundel, BN18-4D 10
High St. Bognor Regis, PO21-5E 23
High St. Bosham, PO18-5A 4
High St. Littlehampton, BN17-2F 27
High St. Selsey, PO20-4C 18
High Trees. PO21-6A 22
Highview Rd. PO20-2C 8
Hilary Rd. PO19-2C 6
Hillfield Rd. PO20-6C 18
Hill La. PO20-5E 9
Hill Rd. BN17-1G 27
Hillsboro Rd. PO21-4D 22
Hillside Cres. BN16-4G 15
Hill Ter. BN18-5B 10
Hillview Cres. BN16-1G 29
Hilton Pk. PO20-3F 17
Hinde Rd. PO22-4B 24
Hislop Wlk. PO21-5E 23
Hobbs Way. BN16-2C 28
Hoe La. PO22-1H 23
  (in two parts)
Holdens Caravan Pk. PO20-4H 17
Holdens, The. PO18-4A 4

Holford Grn. PO20-3E 19
Holland Clo. PO21-3A 22
Hollies, The. PO21-3A 22
Holly Ct. PO22-2D 22
Holly Dri. BN17-5G 13
Holmes La. BN16-3B 28
Holmwood Clo. PO20-2B 16
Homefield Av. PO22-3B 24
Homefield Clo. BN16-1C 28
Homefield Cres. BN18-1G 9
Homelands Av. BN16-3G 29
Homing Gdns. PO22-1C 22
Honer La. PO20-1A 20
Honey La. BN16-4G 15
Hooe, The. BN17-2A 28
Hook La. PO18-6E 5
Hook La. PO20-3A 8
Hook La. PO21-3C 20
  (in two parts)
Hook La. PO22-4E 23
Hopgarton, The. PO21-2G 21
Hornbeam Clo. PO21-6A 22
Hornet Enterprise Cen. PO19-3F 7
Hornet, The. PO19-3F 7
Horns La. PO21-4B 20
Horsefield Rd. PO20-3C 18
Horsemere Grn. La. BN17-2A 26
Horse Shoe, The. PO20-4C 18
Horsham Rd. BN17-2H 27
Horsham Rd. W. BN17-1H 27
Hotham Way. PO22-4E 23
Howard Av. PO20-4C 16
Howard Ho. PO21-4B 22
Howard Pl. BN17-2F 27
Howard Rd. BN17-2E 27
Howard Rd. BN18-5B 10
Howards Way. BN16-4B 28
Huddlestone Clo. BN16-4F 15
Hudson Dri. BN16-3D 28
Hughes Clo. PO21-4A 22
Humber Clo. BN17-3H 27
Hunters Clo. PO21-4E 21
Hunters Race. PO19-4B 2
Hunters Way. PO19-4D 2
Hurst Rd. BN16-1E 29

Icarus Way. PO22-4B 24
Ilex Clo. BN16-3C 28
Ilex Way. PO22-3D 24
Infirmary Ter. PO19-1D 6
Inglewood Clo. PO21-4D 20
Ingram Clo. BN16-2B 28
Innerwyke Clo. PO22-4A 24
Irvine Rd. BN17-3F 27
Island La. PO20-3A 18
Island Loop. PO20-3A 18
Ivanhoe Pl. PO22-4B 24
Ivy Clo. PO20-2A 8
Ivy Cres. PO22-3E 23
Ivydale Rd. PO21-4B 22
Ivy La. PO20-2A 8
Ivy La. PO22-3E 23

James St. PO20-5D 18
Jarvis Rd. BN18-5B 10
Jays Clo. BN17-1F 27
Jays, The. BN17-1F 27
Jeffreys Av. PO19-6E 3
Jervis Av. BN16-3D 28
Jib Clo. BN17-6A 14
John Arundel Rd. PO19-2C 6
Johnson Way. BN18-5H 9
John St. PO21-5E 23
Joliffe Rd. PO20-4C 16
Joyce Clo. BN17-6E 13
Joys Croft. PO19-2F 7
Jubilee Av. BN16-1C 28
Jubilee Pde. PO22-4F 25
Jubilee Rd. PO19-2E 7
Jubilee Ter. PO19-2E 7
Junction Clo. BN18-6H 9
June Clo. PO21-5B 20
Juniper Clo. PO20-3D 24
Juxon Clo. PO19-4E 7

Keats Wlk. PO21-5C 22
Keble Clo. PO21-5A 22
Keelson Way. BN17-1A 28

Keepers Wood. PO19-4D 2
Kendal Clo. BN17-6A 14
Kenhurst. BN16-2G 29
Kenilworth Rd. PO21-4B 22
Kenlegh. PO21-6A 22
Kensington Rd. PO19-3H 7
Kent Rd. BN17-1F 27
Kent Rd. PO19-2F 7
Kestrel Clo. PO20-5F 17
Kestrel Ct. PO19-2H 7
Kestrel Ct. PO21-6B 20
Kestrel Way. BN17-5E 13
Ketch Rd. BN17-3A 28
Kew Gdns. PO21-4A 22
Kilnwood Clo. PO20-4E 19
Kilwich Clo. PO22-3C 24
Kimberry. BN17-6E 13
Kimbridge Rd. PO20-5F 17
Kingfisher Ct. PO22-4E 25
Kings Arms Hill. BN16-4D 10
Kings Av. PO19-5D 6
Kings Clo. BN18-5F 9
Kings Clo. PO20-3D 18
Kings Ct. PO21-4C 22
King's Dri. PO21-5D 20
Kingsham Av. PO19-4F 7
Kingsham Rd. PO19-4E 7
Kingsmead. PO22-4G 23
Kingsmead Gdns. PO22-3F 25
Kingsmead Rd. PO22-3F 25
Kingsmill Rd. PO22-3F 9
King's Pde. PO21-6B 22
Kingston La. BN16-1H 29
King St. BN18-4C 10
Kingsway. PO20-5E 19
Kingsway. PO21-4F 21
Kirdford Clo. BN16-3B 28
Kirdford Rd. BN18-5C 10
Kirkland Clo. BN16-2B 28
Kithurst Clo. BN16-3E 29
Knap La. PO20-4C 18
Knightscroft Av. BN16-3C 28
Knightscroft Clo. BN16-3B 28
Kynon Gdns. PO22-3C 24
Kyoto Ct. PO21-5B 22

Laburnum Gro. PO19-4E 7
Laburnum Gro. PO22-2D 22
Laburnum Wlk. BN16-1B 28
Lacey Ho. PO19-4D 6
Lagoon Rd. PO21-6B 20
Lake La. PO22-3F 9
Lake Rd. PO19-3G 7
Lake View. PO21-4C 20
Lammas Clo. BN17-6G 13
Lamorna Gdns. PO20-3A 8
Lancastrian Grange. PO19-2D 6
Landerry Ind. Est., The. PO20-3C 18
Landseer Dri. PO20-4E 19
Lane End Rd. PO22-4F 25
Lane, The. PO19-5E 3
Langdale Av. PO19-5G 7
Langley Gro. PO21-4E 21
Langton Clo. PO20-5C 18
Langton Rd. PO19-2C 6
Lansdowne Clo. BN16-3F 15
Lansdowne Rd. BN16-4F 15
Lansdowne Rd. BN17-6F 13
Lansdowne Way. BN16-3F 15
Lanyards. BN17-6A 14
Larch Clo. PO19-5D 2
Larch Clo. PO22-1D 22
Larchfield Clo. PO21-4F 21
Large Acres. PO20-4C 18
Lashmar Rd. BN16-2G 29
Latham Rd. PO20-5C 18
Laurel Gro. PO22-2D 22
Lavant Rd. PO18 & PO19-1D 2
Lavant Straight. PO18-2F 3
Lavinia Way. BN16-2G 29
Lawns, The. BN16-3G 29
Lawn, The. PO21-3G 21
Lawrence Av. BN16-1D 28
Layne, The. PO22-4F 25
Leaman Clo. PO22-4E 25
Leander Rd. PO18-4C 4
Leas Ct. PO22-3D 22
Leas, The. BN16-6E 15
Leatherbottle La. PO19-3G 7
Ledbury Way. PO21-3D 20

Ledra Dri. PO21-5D 20
Leecroft. PO21-3G 21
Leeward Rd. BN17-2A 28
Legion Way. PO20-5F 17
Leigh Rd. PO19-4D 6
Leinster Gdns. PO22-5C 24
Lennox Rd. PO19-2F 7
Lennox St. PO21-6E 23
Leonora Dri. PO21-3D 20
Leopold Clo. PO22-3H 23
Leverton Av. PO22-4C 24
Lewes Clo. PO21-4A 22
Lewis Rd. PO19-2F 7
Lewis Rd. PO20-4C 18
Ley Rd. PO22-4A 24
Lichfield Gdns. PO21-2G 21
Lidsey Farm Caravan Camp. PO22
                                    -6A 8
Lidsey Rd. PO20 & PO22-4A 8
Lilac Clo. PO22-3D 24
Lillian Ter. BN18-1C 14
Lime Clo. PO19-2F 7
Lime Gro. BN16-5F 15
Limes, The. BN18-5G 9
Limetree Clo. BN16-1F 29
Limmard Way. PO22-5B 24
Limmer La. PO22-4H 23
Lincoln Av. PO21-1E 21
Lincoln Grn. PO19-6D 2
Linden Pk. BN17-2E 27
Linden Rd. BN17-2E 27
Linden Rd. PO21-4C 22
Lindsey Ct. PO22-2H 23
Lineside Ind. Est. BN17-1D 26
Lineside Way. BN17-1D 26
Lingfield Way. PO20-4E 19
Links Av. PO22-4G 23
Link Way. PO21-4C 20
Lionel Av. PO22-3B 24
Lion Rd. PO21-3C 20
Lion St. PO19-3E 7
Litten Ter. PO19-2E 7
Lit. Babbsham. PO21-3G 21
Lit. Breach. PO19-6D 2
Littlefield Clo. PO20-4E 19
Littlefield Rd. PO19-4F 7
Littlehampton By-Pass. BN17-6D 12
Littlehampton Rd. BN12-6H 15
Lit. High St. PO21-6D 22
Lit. London. PO19-3E 7
Lizard Head. BN17-1A 28
Lloyd Goring Clo. BN16-3F 15
Loats La. PO21-1A 22
Lobster La. PO20-3A 18
Locksash Clo. PO20-1A 16
Lodge Clo. PO22-4F 25
Lodge Ct. PO21-3G 21
Lodsworth Rd. PO21-2D 20
London Rd. BN18-1A 10
            (Arundel)
London Rd. PO21-5E 23
Longacre. PO20-5C 18
Longacre La. PO20-5C 18
Long Brook. PO22-5G 23
Longford Rd. PO21-5D 22
Longlands Rd. PO20-5E 17
Longport Rd. PO22-5A 24
Longships. BN17-1A 28
Loop, The. PO22-5B 24
Loudoun Rd. BN17-1E 27
Lovells Clo. PO21-3D 20
Loveys Rd. BN18-6F 9
Lwr. Bognor Rd. PO20 & PO21-1F 20
Lwr. Hone La. PO18-6A 4
Lower Rd. PO18-2E 3
Loxwood. BN16-6H 15
Lucerne Ct. PO21-3G 21
Lucking La. PO22-4E 25
Ludlow Clo. PO21-3G 21
Lundy Clo. BN17-3A 28
Lyminster Rd. BN17-5F 13
Lyndhurst Rd. PO19-4F 7
Lyon St. PO21-5E 23
Lyon St. W. PO21-5D 22

Mackeral La. PO20-3A 18
Macklin Rd. PO22-4F 23
Madehurst Clo. BN16-3E 29
Madehurst Way. BN17-1F 27
Madeira Av. PO22-4F 23

Madgwick La. PO18-6H 3
Magpie La. PO20-2A 18
Main Dri. PO22-4E 25
Main Rd. BN18-5F 9
Main Rd. PO18-2A 4
Malden Way. PO20-4C 18
Malin Rd. BN17-2A 28
Mallard Cres. PO21-6B 20
Mallon Dene. BN16-3C 28
Malmayne Ct. PO21-5A 22
Malthouse Clo. BN18-5C 10
Malthouse Pas. BN17-1F 27
Malthouse Rd. PO20-4D 18
Maltings, The. PO19-3D 6
Maltravers Dri. BN17-3G 27
Maltravers Rd. BN17-3G 27
Maltravers St. BN18-4D 10
Malvern Way. PO21-4D 20
Manet Sq. PO22-2C 22
Manning Rd. BN17-6E 13
Manning Rd. PO19-1G 7
Manor Clo. BN16-2F 29
Manor Clo. PO19-6D 6
Manor Clo. PO22-4H 23
Manor Farm Clo. PO20-3D 18
Manor Farm Ct. PO20-3D 18
Manor La. PO20-3E 19
Manor Pk. PO21-4C 20
Manor Pl. PO21-6D 22
Manor Rd. BN16-3G 29
  (East Preston)
Manor Rd. BN16-1B 28
  (Rustington)
Manor Rd. PO20-4D 18
Manor Vs. PO18-4C 4
Manor Way. PO21-4D 20
Manor Way. PO22-4G 25
Mansfield Rd. PO22-3C 22
Mantling Rd. BN17-1F 27
Maple Ct. PO22-3D 24
Maple Gdns. PO22-1D 22
Maplehurst Rd. PO19-5F 3
  (in three parts)
Maple Rd. BN18-1H 9
Maple Wlk. BN16-1C 28
Marama Gdns. BN16-4B 28
March Sq. PO19-4E 3
Marchwood. PO19-4E 3
Marchwood M. PO19-4E 3
Marcuse Fields. PO18-3A 4
Marden Av. PO19-6C 6
Margaret Clo. PO21-2G 21
Marian Way. PO21-5F 23
Marine Clo. PO20-5D 16
Marine Dri. PO20-4D 16
  (East Wittering, in two parts)
Marine Dri. PO20-4E 19
  (Selsey)
Marine Dri. W. PO20-4C 16
Marine Gdns. PO20-6C 18
Marine Pde. PO21-6C 22
Mariners Wlk. BN16-3D 28
Marineside. PO20-6G 17
Maris Clo. BN17-3H 27
Marisfield Pl. PO20-3E 19
Market Av. PO19-4E 7
Market Clo. PO22-3E 9
Market Rd. PO19-3E 7
Market St. PO21-6D 22
Markfield. PO22-2C 22
Marlborough Clo. PO19-3H 7
Marlborough Ct. PO21-3A 22
Marlowe Clo. PO22-3D 24
Marshall Av. PO21-4C 22
Marshall Clo. PO22-4E 9
Marsh La. PO18-1D 2
Martello Enterprise Cen. BN17-5E 13
Martlet Clo. PO19-4E 7
Martlets, The. BN16-4A 28
  (in three parts)
Martlet Way. PO21-6B 20
Marylands Cres. PO22-3F 23
Mauldmare Clo. PO21-6A 22
Maxwell Rd. BN17-2E 27
Maxwell Rd. BN18-6B 10
May Clo. PO22-3E 23
Mayfield. BN16-6H 15
Mayfield Clo. PO21-2D 20
Mayfield Rd. PO21-4B 22
Mayflower Way. BN16-6G 15

Mayflower Way. PO19-3F 7
Maynards Camping & Caravan Site.
                                    BN18-6F 11
Maypole La. Caravan Site. BN18-4H 9
Mayridge. PO20-3A 18
Maytree Clo. BN16-5F 15
Mead La. PO22-4E 23
Meadow Ct. PO22-3C 24
Meadowfield Dri. PO19-2G 7
Meadowland. PO20-5C 18
Meadow La. PO20-1C 16
Meadowside. BN16-3G 15
Meadows Rd. PO20-4F 17
Meadows, The. BN18-1H 9
Meadow Wlk. PO22-4F 25
Meadow Way. BN17-2H 27
Meadow Way. PO20-3A 8
Meadow Way. PO21-4D 20
Meadow Way. PO22-2B 22
Meadway. BN16-2D 28
Medmerry. PO20-3A 18
Melbourne Rd. PO19-2F 7
Mendip Clo. BN16-1G 29
Merchant St. PO21-5D 22
Merlin Way. PO22-3C 24
Merrion Av. PO22-3C 22
Merry End. PO22-4C 24
Merryfield Cres. BN16-3G 15
Merryfield Dri. PO20-4E 19
Merryweather Rd. PO18-4B 4
Merton Av. BN16-3D 28
Merton Clo. PO21-1G 21
Merton Dri. BN17-1F 27
Michel Gro. BN16-2E 29
Micklam Clo. PO21-3E 21
Middlefield. PO20-2B 16
Middle Mead. BN17-2A 28
Middleton Rd. PO22-4B 24
Middle Wlk. BN16-3F 29
Midholme. BN16-2F 29
Midhurst Rd. PO18-1C 2
Midway, The. PO22-4H 23
Miles Clo. BN18-6H 9
Miles Cotts. PO18-4C 4
Mill Clo. BN16-1D 28
Mill Clo. PO19-3H 5
Millers Ct. PO21-4D 20
Mill Farm Caravan Pk. PO21-3B 20
Millfield Clo. BN16-4C 28
Millfield Clo. PO19-1G 7
Mill Gdns. PO20-4E 17
Millhouse. PO22-4H 23
Mill La. BN16-1D 28
  (in two parts)
Mill La. BN17-4F 13
  (in two parts)
Mill La. BN18-4D 10
  (Arundel)
Mill La. BN18-1G 9
  (Walberton)
Mill La. PO19-3H 5
Mill La. PO20-4A 18
Mill Pk. Rd. PO21-3C 20
Mill Rd. BN16-4F 15
Mill Rd. BN18-3D 10
Mill Rd. Av. BN16-4F 15
Mill View Rd. BN18-6F 9
Milton Av. BN16-3B 28
Milton Clo. BN16-2B 28
Minton Rd. PO22-4H 23
Mole, The. BN17-2A 28
Mons Av. PO21-3C 22
Montague Rd. PO19-1C 6
Montgomery Dri. PO22-3C 24
Montpelier Rd. BN16-2G 29
Moorhen Way. PO22-2C 22
Moorings, The. BN17-1A 28
Moraunt Dri. PO22-3C 24
Moreton Rd. PO18-4B 4
Mornington Cres. PO22-3H 23
Mosse Gdns. PO19-2H 5
Mountalan Cres. PO20-3A 18
Mountbatten Ct. PO21-6E 23
Mount La. PO19-3D 6
Mt. Pleasant. BN18-4C 10
Mountwood Rd. PO20-3E 19
M'Tongue Av. PO18-2C 4
Mulberry Clo. PO21-6C 20
Mulberry La. PO18-1A 4
Mumford Pl. PO19-5F 7
Munmere Way. BN16-1E 29

Murina Av. PO21-3D 22
Murray Rd. PO20-5C 18
Mustang Clo. BN18-6H 9
Myrtle Gro. BN16-2F 29

Nab Tower La. PO20-3A 18
Nab Wlk. PO20-5E 17
Nagles Clo. PO20-5F 17
Naiad Gdns. PO22-4C 24
Needlemakers. PO19-3F 7
Nelson Rd. PO21-5B 22
Nelson Row. BN18-6A 12
Neptune Ct. PO22-5C 24
Neptune Way. BN17-3A 28
Netherton Clo. PO20-4D 18
Neville Rd. PO19-2B 6
Neville Rd. PO22-4E 23
Newbarn La. PO21-2A 22
   (in two parts)
New Barn La. PO22-3A 24
Newells La. PO18-2A 4
Newfield Rd. PO20-3F 19
Newhall Clo. PO21-5A 22
Newlands La. PO19-1C 6
New Pk. Rd. PO19-2E 7
Newport Dri. PO19-2H 5
New Rd. BN16-6D 14
New Rd. BN17-3F 27
New Ter. BN18-1C 14
New Town. PO19-3E 7
Newtown Av. PO21-2B 22
Nightingale Ct. PO22-4E 25
Nimbus Clo. BN17-1A 28
Nookery, The. BN16-2G 29
Norbren Av. PO21-3B 22
Norfolk Clo. PO21-6C 22
Norfolk Cotts. BN18-1H 11
Norfolk Gdns. BN17-3H 27
Norfolk Pl. BN17-3H 27
Norfolk Rd. BN17-4H 27
Norfolk Sq. PO21-6C 22
Norfolk St. PO21-6E 23
Norfolk Way. PO22-4F 25
Norman Clo. BN17-2H 27
Normandy Dri. BN16-3G 29
Normandy La. BN16-3G 29
Normanhurst Clo. BN16-3C 28
Norman's Dri. PO22-3A 24
Normanton Av. PO21-5C 22
Norris, The. BN16-2H 29
North Av. PO22-4E 25
North Av. E. PO22-4E 25
North Av. S. PO22-4E 25
N. Bersted St. PO22-1B 22
Northcliffe Rd. PO22-4F 23
North Clo. PO19-3E 7
Northcote Rd. PO21-4B 22
Northcourt Clo. BN16-1E 29
North Dri. BN16-5F 15
North End Rd. BN18-5F 9
Northern Cres. PO22-4E 17
Northfield. PO20-4E 19
Northfields La. PO21-1A 8
Northgate. PO19-2E 7
N. Ham Rd. BN17-1F 27
North La. BN16-2G 29
   (East Preston)
North La. BN16-1B 28
   (Rustington)
N. Pallant. PO19-3E 7
North Pl. BN17-3G 27
North Pound. BN18-1G 9
North Rd. PO18-2C 4
North Rd. PO20-4D 18
North Rd. PO22-2H 23
Northside. PO18-1C 2
North St. BN17-5F 13
North St. PO19-3E 7
N. Walls. PO19-3D 6
   (in two parts)
North Way. PO22-4G 23
Northway Rd. BN17-5F 13
Northwyke Clo. PO22-4B 24
Northwyke Rd. PO22-4B 24
Norway La. BN17-6H 13
Norwich Rd. PO19-1D 6
Nuffield Clo. PO21-2G 21
Nunnington Farm Caravan Pk. PO20
   -1C 16
Nursery Clo. BN16-3G 29

Nursery Clo. PO22-3E 9
Nursery Gdns. BN17-6F 13
Nursery La. PO19-2H 5
Nytember Clo. PO21-3D 20
Nytember Cres. PO21-3D 20
Nytember La. PO21-3C 20
Nytember Mill. PO21-3C 20
Nytembers, The. PO21-3C 20
Nyewood Gdns. PO21-5C 22
Nyewood La. PO21-4C 22
Nyewood Pl. PO21-6C 22
Nyton Rd. PO20-1A 8

Oak Av. PO19-2C 6
Oak Clo. PO19-2C 6
Oak Clo. PO22-2D 22
Oakcroft Gdns. BN17-6H 13
Oak End. BN18-5A 10
Oakfield Av. PO20-4E 17
Oakfield Rd. PO20-4E 17
Oak Gro. PO22-2D 22
Oakhurst Gdns. BN16-1E 29
Oaklands Clo. PO19-1D 6
Oaklands Way. PO19-2E 7
Oakley Gdns. BN16-2G 29
Oaks Clo. PO20-3A 8
Oaks, The. BN16-2E 29
Oak Trees La. PO20-4A 8
Oakwood Gdns. PO21-4D 22
Ockley Ct. PO21-5D 22
Ockley Rd. PO21-5D 22
Old Bakery La. PO21-6D 22
Old Bri. Rd. PO18-2C 4
Old Broyle Rd. PO19-5A 2
Old Canal Caravan Site. PO22-6A 8
Old Coastguards. PO22-4G 23
Older Way. BN16-3F 15
Old Farm Clo. PO21-3F 21
Oldlands Way. PO22-1F 23
Old Manor Ho. Gdns. PO22-4A 24
Old Mnr. Rd. BN16-1B 28
Old Mkt. Av. PO19-3E 7
Old Mead Rd. BN17-4E 13
Old Park La. PO18-3G 5
Old Pl. PO21-2G 21
Old Point. PO22-5D 24
Old Rectory Dri. PO20-2B 8
Old Rectory Gdns. PO22-4H 23
Old Worthing Rd. BN16-6H 15
Olivers Meadow. PO20-2A 8
Oliver Whitby Rd. PO19-2B 6
Olivia Ct. PO21-6C 22
Olivier Ct. PO21-2B 22
Orchard Av. PO19-2D 6
Orchard Av. PO20-5D 18
Orchard Caravan Pk. PO21-1A 22
Orchard Clo. PO21-5C 22
Orchard Gdns. BN16-1D 28
Orchard Gdns. PO19-2D 6
Orchard Gdns. PO20-4A 8
Orchard Pk. Caravan Site. BN16-6B 14
Orchard Pl. BN18-4D 10
Orchard Rd. BN16-1F 6A 14
Orchard St. PO19-3D 6
Orchard, The. PO21-4E 21
Orchard Way. PO22-3E 9
   (Barnham)
Orchard Way. PO22-3D 22
   (Bognor Regis)
Oriel Clo. PO22-3E 9
Orme Cotts. BN16-3F 15
Ormesby Cres. PO22-3H 23
Ormonde Av. PO19-3F 7
Orpen Pl. PO20-4E 19
Osborn Cres. PO19-6E 3
Osborne Cres. PO19-3H 7
Osprey Clo. BN17-5F 13
Osprey Gdns. PO22-1D 22
Otard Clo. PO19-2D 6
Otter Clo. PO19-1C 6
Otway Rd. PO19-5E 3
Outerwyke Av. PO22-2H 23
Outerwyke Gdns. PO22-3A 24
Outerwyke Rd. PO22-2H 23
Outram Rd. PO22-5G 23
Overdown Rd. PO22-4A 24
Overstrand Av. BN16-3B 28
Oving Rd. PO19-3G 7
Oving Ter. PO19-3G 7
Owers Way. PO20-4D 16

Oxford Clo. PO20-3E 17
Oxford Dri. PO21-1G 21
Oxford St. PO21-6C 22

Paddock Grn. BN16-1E 29
Paddock La. PO20-4C 18
Paddocks. PO22-3E 9
Paddocks, The. BN17-3E 13
Paddock, The. PO22-3D 22
Pagham Rd. PO21-5B 20
Palm Ct. BN16-3G 29
Palmer Rd. BN16-3F 15
Parade, The. BN16-3G 29
Parade, The. PO21-5C 20
Parchment St. PO19-2D 6
Parham Clo. BN16-3B 28
Parham Clo. BN17-1F 27
Park Av. PO20-4E 19
Park Copse. PO20-2G 19
Park Cres. PO20-3F 19
Park Dri. BN16-1D 28
Park Dri. BN18-6G 9
Park Dri. PO22-4C 24
Parker's Cotts. PO18-1E 3
Parkfield Av. PO21-2F 21
Parklands Av. PO21-4C 22
Parklands Rd. PO19-3C 6
Park La. PO18-6E 5
   (Bosham)
Park La. PO18-3B 2
   (Chichester)
Park La. PO20-2E 19
Park Pl. BN18-4C 10
Park Rd. BN18-6G 9
Park Rd. PO20-3F 19
Park Rd. PO21-6C 22
Park Rd. PO22-3G 9
Parkside Av. BN17-2H 27
Parkside Ct. BN17-2H 27
Park Ter. PO21-6C 22
Parkway. PO21-5B 22
Parkway, The. BN16-2D 28
Parry Dri. BN16-2B 28
Parson's Hill. BN18-4D 10
Parsons Wlk. BN18-1H 9
Paterson Wilson Rd. BN17-1G 27
Payne Clo. PO21-5C 20
Peacheries, The. PO19-4G 7
Peachey Rd. PO20-5C 18
Peak La. BN16-3H 29
Pearson Rd. BN18-5B 10
Peckhams Copse La. PO20-6H 7
Peel Cen., The. PO22-1E 23
Peel Clo. BN17-1E 27
Peerley Clo. PO20-5F 17
Peerley Rd. PO20-5F 17
Pembroke Way. PO21-1G 21
Penfold La. BN16-6C 14
Penfolds Pl. BN18-5C 10
Penn Clo. PO22-4D 24
Pennyfields. PO22-4B 24
Penwarden Way. PO18-2C 4
Pepple Wlk. BN17-6A 14
Peregrine Rd. BN17-1H 27
Peterhouse Clo. PO21-4A 22
Peter's La. PO20-3A 18
Peter's Pl. PO20-3A 18
Pevensey Rd. PO21-4A 22
Phillips Bus. Cen. PO19-4C 6
Phoenix Clo. PO19-4E 7
Pier Rd. BN17-3F 27
Pigeonhouse La. BN16-3E 29
Piggery Hall La. PO20-2E 17
Pilgrims Way. PO21-4D 20
Pine Gro. PO19-6A 2
Pinehurst Pk. PO21-1F 21
Pines, The. BN16-5F 15
Pines, The. BN18-5F 9
Pine Trees Clo. BN16-2F 15
Pine Wlk. PO21-1F 21
Pinewood Clo. BN16-1G 29
Pinewood Gdns. PO21-5B 22
Pitcroft, The. PO19-1G 7
Place St Maur des Fosses. PO21-6E 23
   (off Belmont St.)
Plainwood Clo. PO19-5D 2
Plantation, The. BN16-2G 29
Plover Clo. PO20-5F 17
Plover Clo. PO22-1C 22
Poling St. BN18-3A 14

Pond Rd. PO20-6G 17
Pontins S. Downs. PO20-4G 17
Pook La. PO18-2D 2
Poplars Caravan Pk. PO22-1E 23
   (Rowan Way)
Poplars Caravan Pk., The. PO22-2E 23
   (Shripney Rd.)
Portfield Way. PO19-1G 7
Portland Clo. BN17-1A 28
Portsmouth Rd. PO18 PO1-3F 5
Portsmouth Rd. PO19-3G 5
Potters Mead. BN17-6E 13
Poulner Clo. PO22-3H 23
Pound Farm Rd. PO19-3G 7
Pound Rd. BN18-1G 9
Pound Rd. PO20-2A 16
Pound, The. PO21-3G 21
Poyntz Clo. PO19-6D 6
Prawn Clo. PO20-3B 18
Precinct, The. PO21-4A 22
Preston Av. BN16-2D 28
Preston Paddock. BN16-2E 29
Priestley Way. PO22-4C 24
Prime Clo. BN18-1H 9
Princes Croft. PO21-4C 20
Princes Marina Ho. BN17-4C 28
Princess Av. PO21-6B 22
Priors Waye. PO21-3C 20
Priory Clo. PO21-5D 20
Priory Rd. BN16-1B 28
Priory Rd. BN18-6B 10
Priory Rd. PO19-2E 7
Promenade. PO21 & PO22-5H 23
Promenade, The. BN17-4G 27
Providence, The. PO19-2D 6
Pryors Grn. PO21-3E 21
Pryors La. PO21-4E 21
Pulborough Way. PO22-3C 24
Purbeck Pl. BN17-2E 27
Pyrford Clo. PO21-3D 20

Quarry La. PO19-4G 7
Quarry La. Ind. Est. PO19-4G 7
Quayside. PO21-2D 26
Queen's Av. PO19-5D 6
Queen's Fields E. PO21-4A 22
Queens Fields Wlk. PO21-4A 22
Queen's Fields W. PO21-1G 21
   (in two parts)
Queens Gdns. PO19-5D 6
Queens La. BN18-5D 10
Queensmead. PO21-5B 20
Queen's Sq. PO21-5E 23
Queen St. BN17-2F 27
Queen St. BN18-4D 10
Queensway. PO21-4G 21
   (Aldwick)
Queensway. PO21-5D 22
   (Bognor Regis)

Rackham Rd. BN16-4B 28
Radford Rd. PO21-3C 22
Raleigh Rd. PO21-2D 20
Ramilies Gdns. PO22-4B 24
Ranworth Rd. PO22-3G 23
Ratham La. PO18-1C 4
Raughmere Ct. PO18-2D 2
Raughmere Dri. PO18-3D 2
Ravens Way. PO22-2C 22
Raycroft Clo. PO21-6A 22
Rayden Clo. BN17-2G 27
Rectory La. BN16-4F 15
Rectory La. PO19-1E 19
Redhouse Farm Caravan Site. PO20
   -2H 17
Redwing Clo. BN17-5E 13
Redwood Ct. BN17-2G 27
Redwood Pl. PO21-3G 21
Reef Clo. BN17-3H 27
Regents Way. PO21-4A 22
Regis Av. PO21-5D 20
Regis Ct. PO21-5E 23
Regnum Cotts. PO19-5E 3
Renoir Ct. PO22-2B 22
Renoir M. PO22-2B 22
Rew La. PO19-4D 2
Richmond Av. PO19-6E 3
Richmond Av. PO21-5B 22
Richmond Av. W. PO21-6B 22

Richmond Clo. BN16-1E 29
Richmond Rd. PO21-5D 22
Richmond Rd. N. PO21-4E 23
Ridgeway, The. PO22-5A 24
Ridings, The. BN16-3F 29
Ridings, The. PO21-4E 21
Rife La. PO20-3A 18
Rife Way. PO22-4G 23
Ripon Gdns. PO21-2G 21
River Rd. BN17-2E 27
River Rd. BN18-5D 10
Riverside. PO19-2F 7
Riverside Caravan Cen. PO22-1E 23
Riverside Ind. Est. BN17-1D 26
Robin Clo. BN17-5E 13
Robin's Clo. PO20-3D 18
Robins Dri. PO21-2F 21
Rochester Clo. PO19-6D 2
Rochester Way. PO21-2G 21
Rockall Clo. BN17-1B 28
Rock Gdns. PO21-6D 22
Rodney Clo. PO21-2E 21
Rodney Cres. BN18-5A 12
Rollaston Pk. BN18-6H 9
Roman Acre. BN17-1E 27
Roman Landing. PO20-1A 16
Roman Way. PO19-3H 5
Romney Broadwalk. PO22-2C 22
Romney Garth. PO20-4E 19
Rookwood Rd. PO20-1B 16
Rope Wlk. BN17-2E 27
Rose Av. PO22-4E 25
Rose Cotts. PO22-4E 9
Rose Green Rd. PO21-2E 21
Rossalyn Clo. PO21-2D 20
Ross Clo. PO21-3D 20
Rosvara Av. PO20-2A 8
Roundle Av. PO22-3A 24
Roundle Rd. PO22-4B 24
Roundle Sq. PO22-4A 24
Roundle Sq. Rd. PO22-4A 24
Round Piece. PO20-3B 18
Round Piece La. PO20-3A 18
Roundstone By-Pass. BN16-6F 15
Roundstone Cres. BN16-1F 29
Roundstone Dri. BN16-1F 29
*Roundstone Ho. Caravan Pk. BN16
(off Old Worthing Rd.)   -6H 15*
Roundstone La. BN16-4G 15
Roundstone Way. PO20-3E 19
Roundway, The. BN16-3D 28
Rowan Way. PO22-1C 22
Royal Clo. PO19-3G 7
Royce Clo. PO20-2B 16
Royce Way. PO20-2B 16
Roystons, The. BN16-3F 29
Rucrofts Clo. PO21-5A 22
Rudgwick Clo. BN16-3B 28
Rudwick's Clo. PO22-5B 24
Rudwick's Way. PO22-5B 24
Ruislip Gdns. PO21-3E 21
Rumbolds Clo. PO19-4G 7
Runnymede Ct. PO21-3A 22
Rusbridge Clo. PO21-1F 21
Ruskin Clo. PO20-4E 19
Russell Rd. PO20-4D 16
Russell's Clo. BN16-1H 29
Russell St. PO19-3G 7
Rustington By-Pass. BN17 & BN16
                                     -6H 13
Rustington Trading Est. BN16-6C 14
Ruston Av. BN16-2D 28
Ruston Pk. BN16-2E 29
Rutland Way. PO18-1H 7
Rydal Clo. BN17-1A 28

Saddle La. PO20-3C 18
Sadler St. PO21-6D 22
St Anthony's Wlk. PO21-2F 21
St Anthonys Way. BN16-1D 28
St Augustine Rd. BN17-3G 27
St Bartholomews Clo. PO19-3C 6
St Catherine's Rd. BN17-3F 27
St Claire Ter. PO21-5D 22
St Clare's Gdns. PO21-2B 22
St Cyriacs. PO19-2E 7
St Flora's Rd. BN17-2H 27
St George's Clo. PO20-3E 19
St George's Dri. PO19-6D 6
St Georges Wlk. PO20-2C 8

St Itha Clo. PO20-4D 18
St Itha Rd. PO20-5D 18
St James's Ind. Est. PO19-2G 7
St James's Rd. PO19-2G 7
St James's Sq. PO19-2G 7
St John's Clo. PO20-4A 8
St John's Clo. PO21-4A 22
St Johns St. PO19-3E 7
St Margarets Ct. BN16-3F 15
St Martin's La. BN17-2F 27
St Martin's Rd. BN17-2F 27
St Martins Sq. PO19-2E 7
St Martins St. PO19-3E 7
St Marys Clo. PO21-2G 27
St Mary's Clo. PO22-3E 23
St Mary's Dri. BN16-2F 29
St Marys Gdns. BN17-2G 27
St Marys Gdns. PO19-3E 7
St Marys Way. BN17-2G 27
St Nicholas Ct. PO22-4E 25
St Nicholas La. PO22-4E 25
St Nicholas Rd. PO18-1C 2
St Pancras. PO19-3F 7
St Paul's Gdns. PO19-2D 6
St Paul's Rd. PO19-1C 6
St Peters. PO19-2E 7
St Peters Clo. PO21-1G 21
St Peter's Cres. PO20-3D 18
St Richard's Dri. PO21-2F 21
St Richards Rd. PO20-2B 8
St Richard's Wlk. PO19-3D 6
St Richard's Way. PO21-2F 21
St Thomas Ct. PO21-5C 20
St Thomas Dri. PO21-5B 20
St Wilfred's Clo. PO20-3F 19
St Wilfrid Rd. PO19-2B 6
St Winefride's Rd. BN17-3G 27
St Winifred's Clo. PO21-6C 22
Salisbury Way. PO19-6D 2
Salthill La. PO19-1A 6
Salthill Rd. PO19-3H 5
Saltings, The. BN17-1A 28
Sandfield Av. BN17-5F 13
Sandpiper Ct. PO20-5F 17
Sandringham Clo. PO20-6G 17
Sandringham Rd. PO19-3H 7
Sandringham Way. PO21-4C 22
Sandymount Av. PO22-3C 22
Sandymount Clo. PO22-2D 22
Sandy Point La. PO20-3A 18
Sandy Rd. PO21-6C 20
Sarisbury Clo. PO22-3H 23
Satinwood Clo. PO22-3D 24
Saxon Clo. BN16-6H 15
Saxon Clo. PO21-5B 20
School La. BN18-5D 10
School La. PO18-4C 4
School La. PO20-2B 8
  (Eastergate)
School La. PO20-3C 18
  (Selsey)
Schooner Ct. BN17-1A 28
Scott Clo. PO21-6D 22
Scotts Farm Caravan Pk. PO20-3D 16
Scott St. PO21-6D 22
Sea Av. BN16-3D 28
Sea Clo. PO22-4D 24
Seacourt Clo. PO21-4F 21
Sea Dri. PO22-5B 24
Seafield Clo. BN16-3C 28
Seafield Clo. PO20-5F 17
Seafield Rd. BN16-5F 29
  (East Preston)
Seafield Rd. BN16-3B 28
  (Rustington)
Seafields. PO20-6G 17
Seafield Way. PO20-5F 17
Seaford Clo. BN17-3H 27
Seagate Ct. PO20-5D 16
Seagate Wlk. BN17-3A 28
Seagull Clo. PO20-2A 18
Sea La. BN16-3F 29
  (East Preston)
Sea La. BN16-4B 28
  (Rustington)
Sea La. PO21-5B 20
Sea La. PO22-4D 24
Sea La. BN16-2F 29
Seal Rd. PO20-5C 18
Seal Sq. PO20-6C 18
Sea Rd. BN16-2G 29

Sea Rd. BN17 & BN16-4H 27
Sea Rd. PO20-5D 18
Seaton Clo. BN17-5F 13
Seaton La. BN17-5F 13
Seaton Pk. BN17-5F 13
Seaton Rd. BN17-5F 13
Seaview Av. BN16-3G 29
  (East Preston)
Seaview Ct. PO20-6C 18
Seaview Gdns. BN16-3C 28
Seaview Rd. BN16-3G 29
Seaward Dri. PO20-2B 16
Seawaves Clo. BN16-2G 29
Sea Way. PO21-5B 20
Sea Way. PO22-4G 25
  (Elmer)
Sea Way. PO22-5C 24
  (Middleton-on-Sea)
Second Av. PO20-6G 17
Second Av. PO22-5A 24
Sefter Rd. PO21-1D 20
Sefton Av. PO21-2F 21
Selborne Rd. BN17-3G 27
Selborne Way. BN16-2F 29
Selden La. BN13-1H 15
Selham Clo. PO19-4E 3
Selhurst Clo. BN16-2F 29
Selsey Av. PO21-6B 22
Selsey Rd. PO19-6C 6
Selsey Rd. PO20-6F 7
Selway La. BN17-1H 27
Selwyn Av. BN17-6F 13
Selwyn Clo. PO21-4A 22
Servite Clo. PO21-4C 22
Sextant Ct. BN17-1A 28
Shaftesbury Ct. BN16-3C 28
Shaftesbury Rd. BN16-3C 28
Shalbourne Cres. PO20-6H 17
Shamrock Clo. PO18-4C 4
Shamrock Clo. PO19-1F 7
  (in two parts)
Shannon Clo. BN17-3A 28
Shardeloes Rd. BN16-3F 15
Shaw Clo. PO22-4E 25
Shearwater Dri. PO22-2D 22
Sheep Fold Av. BN16-1E 29
Sheepwash La. PO18-2D 2
Shelley Rd. PO21-5C 22
Sherborne Rd. PO19-3C 6
Sherbourne La. PO20-3A 18
Sherlock Av. PO19-2C 6
Sherwood Clo. PO22-2B 22
Sherwood Rd. PO22-2C 22
Shingle Wlk. PO20-5E 17
Shipfield. PO21-6A 22
Shirley Clo. BN16-3D 28
Shirley Clo. PO21-5C 20
Shirley Dri. PO22-2H 23
Shirleys Garden. PO22-4A 24
Shopfield Clo. BN16-1C 28
Shop La. PO18-2E 3
Shopwyke Rd. PO20-2H 7
Shorecroft. PO21-4H 21
Shore Rd. PO18-5A 4
Shore Rd. PO20-5D 16
Shoreside Wlk. PO20-5E 17
Short Furlong. BN17-2H 27
Shripney La. PO22-1C 22
Shripney Rd. PO22-3E 23
  (in two parts)
Shrubbs Dri. PO22-4D 24
Silver Birch. PO22-3D 24
Silverdale Clo. PO21-5C 20
Silverston Av. PO21-6B 22
Silver Way. PO20-6H 17
Singleton Clo. PO21-4D 20
Slattsfield Clo. PO20-4E 19
Snakes La. PO18-3C 2
Solent Clo. BN17-6A 14
Solent Rd. PO20-5E 17
Solent Way. PO20-6C 18
Solway Clo. BN17-2A 28
Somerset Gdns. PO21-3D 22
Somerset Rd. BN16-1H 29
Somerstown. PO19-2D 6
Somerton Grn. PO22-3G 23
South Av. PO21-5A 22
S. Bank. PO19-5D 6
S. Bersted Ind. Est. PO22-2E 23
S. Coast World. PO21-5F 23
Southcote Av. PO20-4D 16

Southcourt Clo. BN16-1E 29
Southdean Clo. PO22-4E 25
Southdean Dri. PO22-4E 25
Southdown Rd. PO21-5D 22
South Dri. BN16-6D 14
South Dri. PO22-4B 24
Southern Cross Ind. Est. PO22-1F 23
Southern Rd. PO20-5D 18
Southfield Ind. Pk. PO18-3B 4
Southfields Clo. PO19-6D 6
Southfields Rd. BN17-2H 27
South Ga. PO19-4D 6
Southover Rd. PO21-5D 22
S. Pallant. PO19-3E 7
South Pas. BN17-3G 27
South Rd. PO22-3G 23
S. Strand. BN16-3G 29
South St. PO19-3E 7
South Ter. BN17-3F 27
  (in two parts)
South Ter. PO18-2C 4
S. View. BN16-3H 29
Southview Rd. PO22-5A 24
South Vs. PO18-2C 4
South Wlk. BN16-4E 29
South Wlk. PO22-4C 24
Southwark Wlk. PO21-1G 21
Southway. BN17-3H 27
South Way. PO21-3B 22
Sparks Ct. BN17-2F 27
Spencer St. PO21-5E 23
Spinnaker Clo. BN17-2A 28
Spinney, The. BN16-3G 29
Spinney, The. PO21-2G 21
Spinney Wlk. PO22-3E 9
Spitalfield La. PO19-2E 7
Springbank. PO19-6D 2
Springfield. PO21-3C 20
Springfield Clo. BN16-2E 29
Springfield Clo. PO18-1C 2
Sproule Clo. BN18-6H 9
Spur Rd. PO19-4H 7
Square, The. BN16-4F 15
Stablefield. PO22-4G 25
Staffords Clo. BN16-1B 28
Stalham Way. PO22-2H 23
Stanbrok Clo. PO21-2G 21
Stanbury Clo. PO18-2C 4
Stanford Clo. PO22-3F 23
Stanhope Rd. BN17-2G 27
Stanley Clo. PO21-4E 23
Stanley Ct. PO22-3C 24
Stanley Rd. BN17-6F 13
Stanmore Gdns. PO21-3G 21
Stanover La. PO22-1G 23
  (in two parts)
Stansfield Ct. BN17-4F 13
Stanton Dri. PO19-4D 2
Staple La. PO18-1E 3
Stapleton Ct. PO21-2F 21
Starboard Wlk. BN17-3H 27
Station Pde. BN16-1E 29
Station Rd. BN16-1D 28
Station Rd. BN18-5E 11
Station Rd. PO18-2C 4
Station Rd. PO21-5D 22
Staveley Gdns. PO19-4D 2
Stean Furlong. BN17-6E 13
Stempswood Way. PO22-3F 9
Sternway. BN17-2A 28
Stewards Rise. BN18-6B 10
Steyne St. PO21-5D 22
  (in two parts)
Steyne, The. PO21-6D 22
Steyning Way. PO22-1F 23
Stirling Rd. PO19-3E 7
Stirling Way. PO21-3G 21
Stockbridge Gdns. PO19-6C 6
Stockbridge Rd. PO19-5D 6
Stocker Rd. PO21-6C 22
Stocks La. PO18-3F 3
Stocks La. PO20-4D 16
  (in two parts)
Stoneage Clo. PO22-1D 22
Stonefields. BN16-2D 28
Stonehill Cres. PO21-2D 20
Stoney Stile La. PO21-4E 21
Stonystile Clo. PO21-3E 21
Storrington Clo. PO19-2H 5
Story Rd. PO19-2G 7

Strand E., The. PO20-3B 16
Strand Way. PO22-5A 24
Strand W., The. PO20-3A 16
Strange Garden. PO21-4H 21
Stratton Ct. PO22-3F 23
Stream Clo. PO18-4B 4
Street, The. BN16-2F 29
(East Preston)
Street, The. BN16-2B 28
(Rustington)
Street, The. BN18-1H 9
Stroud Grn. Dri. PO21-3A 22
Stubcroft La. PO20-5G 17
Stumps End. PO18-5C 4
Stumps La. PO18-5C 4
Sturges Rd. PO21-5D 22
Sudbury Clo. PO21-4E 21
Sudley Gdns. PO21-5E 23
Sudley Rd. PO21-5E 23
Summerfield Rd. PO20-1A 16
Summerhill Clo. PO22-3B 24
Summerhill Dri. PO22-3B 24
Summer La. PO21-4B 20
Summerlea Gdns. BN17-2G 27
Summerley La. PO22-4A 24
Summersdale Ct. PO19-4D 2
Summersdale Rd. PO19-6E 3
Sundale La. PO22-4D 24
Sunningdale Gdns. PO20-4C 16
Sunningdale Gdns. PO22-1C 22
Sunnymead Clo. PO20-5E 19
Sunnymead Dri. PO22-3F 25
Sunnymead Rd. PO20-5D 18
Sunny Way. PO18-4B 4
Sun Pk. Clo. PO21-2B 22
Surrey St. BN18-5C 10
Surrey St. BN17-2F 27
Surrey St. BN18-5C 10
Surrey Wharf. BN18-5D 10
Sussex Ct. PO22-4G 25
Sussex Dri. PO21-4C 20
Sussex Gdns. BN16-1C 28
Sussex St. BN17-1F 27
Sussex St. PO21-5E 23
Sussex Village. PO22-4G 25
(off Manor Way)
Sutherland Clo. BN16-2B 28
Sutherland Clo. PO21-5D 22
Sutton Av. BN16-3C 28
Sutton Clo. PO22-2G 23
Swanbourne. BN17-6F 13
Swan Dene. PO21-6B 20
Swanfield Dri. PO19-2F 7
Swansea Gdns. PO21-6C 22
Swift Way. BN17-5E 13
Swillage La. BN13-1G 15
Sycamore Clo. BN16-5F 15
Sycamore Rd. PO22-1D 22
Sylvan Way. PO21-5C 22
Sylvia Clo. PO21-4C 20

Tabard Ga. PO21-4D 20
Tack Lee Rd. BN18-5F 9
Talbot Rd. BN17-2E 27
Tamarisk Clo. PO22-2D 22
Tamarisk Wlk. PO20-5D 16
Tamarisk Way. BN16-3E 29
Tangmere Gdns. PO21-3F 21
Tarrant St. BN18-5D 10
Tarrant Wharf. BN18-5D 10
Tasman Clo. BN16-3D 28
Taverner Pl. PO19-4F 7
Taylor's La. PO18-5C 4
Templars Clo. PO22-3C 24
Temple Sheen Rd. PO22-4G 25
Tenacre Clo. PO19-1F 7
Tennyson Av. BN16-2A 28
Tennyson Rd. PO21-5B 22
Terminus Ind. Est. PO19-4C 6
Terminus Pl. BN17-2F 27
Terminus Rd. BN17-2E 27
Terminus Rd. PO19-4B 6
Terrace, The. BN18-1G 13
Thakeham Clo. BN16-5H 15
Thames Clo. BN17-3A 28
Thatchway Clo. BN17-1F 27
Thatchway, The. BN16-4E 15
(Angmering)
Thatchway, The. BN16-3D 28
(Rustington)

Theatre La. PO19-3E 7
Thicketts, The. PO21-1E 21
Third Av. PO20-6G 17
Third Av. PO22-5B 24
Thirlmere Way. PO22-3A 24
Thorgate Rd. BN17-6D 12
Thorncroft Rd. BN17-1G 27
Thorndene Av. PO21-4C 22
Thorney Dri. PO20-4B 18
Thornlea Caravan Pk. BN17-4E 13
Thrusloes. PO21-4H 21
Tideway. BN17-3A 28
Tile Barn La. PO20-2H 17
Timberleys. BN17-6H 13
Tinghall. PO21-2G 21
Tithe Barn Chalets. PO20-3A 18
(off Montalan Cres.)
Tithe Barn Clo. PO21-4E 21
Tithe Barn Ct. PO21-4D 20
Tithe Barn Way. PO21-4D 20
Tithe Grn. BN16-2B 28
Toddington La. BN17-5F 13
Tollhouse Clo. PO19-3D 6
Torton Hill Rd. BN18-5B 10
Tower Clo. PO19-2D 6
Tower Ho. Gdns. BN18-4D 10
Tower Pl. PO20-4E 17
Tower Rd. PO20-4E 17
Tower St. PO19-2D 6
Town Cross Av. PO21-4D 22
Townsend Cres. BN17-1H 27
Tozer Way. PO19-3F 7
Tregarth Rd. PO19-5E 3
Trendle Grn. PO21-5A 22
Tretawn Gdns. PO20-5E 19
Trinity Way. BN17-3H 27
Trinity Way. PO21-4A 22
Triton Pl. PO22-4B 24
Trotyn Croft. PO21-5A 22
True Blue Precinct. BN17-6F 13
Trundle Clo. PO18-1C 2
Trundle View Clo. PO22-3E 9
Truro Clo. PO19-6D 2
Truro Cres. PO21-2G 21
Tryndel Way. PO22-5A 24
Tudor Clo. PO19-5D 2
Tudor Clo. PO22-4C 24
Turnbull Rd. PO19-2F 7
Turner Way. PO20-4E 19
Turnpike Clo. PO19-6C 6
Tuscan Av. PO22-4E 25
Tyne Way. PO21-1F 21
Tythe Barn Rd. PO20-5D 18

Ullswater Dri. BN17-6A 14
Ullswater Gro. PO22-3A 24
Uppark Way. PO22-3C 24
Up. Bognor Rd. PO22 & PO21-4E 23
(in two parts)
Upper Dri. BN16-3H 29
Upton Rd. PO19-5D 2
Upways Clo. PO20-2D 18
Ursula Av. PO20-5C 18
Ursula Av. N. PO20-5C 18
Ursula Sq. PO20-6C 18

Valentines Gdns. PO21-3E 21
Van Dyck Pl. PO22-2B 22
Van Gogh Pl. PO22-2C 22
Velyn Av. PO19-3F 7
Venus La. PO21-6A 20
Vermont Dri. BN16-2G 29
Vermont Way. BN16-2G 29
Vernon Clo. BN16-2C 28
Veronica Clo. BN16-2C 28
Vicarage La. BN16-2F 29
Vicarage La. PO22-4G 23
Vicars Clo. PO19-3D 6
Victoria Dri. PO21-6C 22
Victoria Gdns. PO20-2A 8
Victoria Rd. PO19-3G 7
Victoria Rd. PO21-6C 22
Victoria Rd. S. PO21-6C 22
View, The. PO17-5C 20
Villa Pl. PO22-4F 25
Vincent Rd. PO20-5B 18
Vinnetrow Rd. PO20-4H 7
Viscount Dri. PO21-5D 20

Wade End. PO20-3B 18
Wadeway. PO20-3B 18
Wadeway Caravan Site. PO20-3B 18
Wadeway, The. PO20-3B 18
Wadhurst Clo. PO21-4C 22
Wad, The. PO20-2A 16
Wakefield Way. PO21-1G 21
Wakehurst Pl. BN16-1C 28
Walberton Clo. PO22-3H 23
Walders Rd. BN16-1B 28
Wallace Rd. BN16-6C 14
Wallfield. PO21-4H 21
Wallner Cres. PO22-4B 24
Walmsleys Way. PO20-6H 17
Walnut Av. BN16-2B 28
Walnut Av. PO19-1C 6
Walnut Tree Caravan Pk. PO20-1B 16
Walsham Clo. PO22-2G 23
Walton Av. PO21-5F 23
Walton La. PO18-4C 4
Walton Rd. PO21-5E 23
Wansford Way. PO22-5B 24
Warblers Way. PO22-1C 22
Warner Rd. PO20-5B 18
Warner's La. PO20-3A 18
Warningcamp La. BN18-4G 11
Warren Cres. BN16-1F 29
Warren Farm La. PO19-5D 2
Warren Way. PO22-3E 9
Warwick Clo. PO21-3D 20
Warwick Pl. PO22-4C 24
Washington St. PO19-2D 6
Water La. BN16-4F 15
Water La. BN17-1F 27
Waterloo Rd. PO22-4H 23
Waterloo Sq. PO21-6D 22
Watermead Bus. Pk. BN17-5H 13
Waterplat, The. PO19-1F 7
Waters Edge. PO21-4G 21
Waterside Dri. PO19-6D 6
Watersmead Bus. Pk. BN17-5H 13
Watersmeet. PO19-3A 6
Watery La. PO19-6E 7
Waverley Rd. BN16-2C 28
Waverley Rd. PO21-4B 22
Way, The. BN16-3G 29
Weavers Hill. BN16-4G 15
Weavers Ring. BN16-4G 15
Webb Clo. PO21-6C 20
Wedgwood Rd. PO22-4H 23
Wellington Gdns. PO20-3D 18
Wellington Rd. PO19-6E 3
Wellington Rd. PO21-5C 22
Well Rd. PO21-6B 20
Wells Cres. PO19-6D 2
Wells Cres. PO21-2F 21
Wellsfield. PO20-2B 16
Wendy Ridge. BN16-1B 28
Wentworth Clo. PO22-2E 9
Wessex Av. PO20-4F 17
Wessex Av. PO21-6B 22
West Av. PO21-5A 22
West Av. PO22-3E 25
W. Beach. PO20-4C 16
W. Beach Caravan Pk. BN17-3E 27
W. Beach Rd. PO20-4C 16
W. Bracklesham Dri. PO20-5F 17
Westbridge Path. PO18-3C 2
Westbrook Clo. PO18-4A 4
Westbrook Field. PO18-4A 4
W. Broyle Dri. PO19-5A 2
West Clo. PO22-5A 24
(Felpham)
West Clo. PO22-4C 24
(Middleton-on-Sea)
West Dri. BN16-5D 14
West Dri. PO21-4D 20
West Dri. PO22-4F 25
Westergate St. PO20-4A 8
Western Rd. BN17-3G 27
Western Rd. PO20-5D 18
W. Front Rd. PO21-6B 20
Westgate. PO21-6D 22
Westhampnett Rd. PO19 & PO18
                              -2G 7
W. Head. BN17-3H 27
Westingway. PO21-1G 21
Westlands. BN17 & BN16-1A 28
Westloats Gdns. PO21-3C 22

Westloats La. PO21-3B 22
W. Mead. BN16-3E 29
Westmead Rd. PO19-3A 6
W. Meads Dri. PO21-3A 22
Westminster Dri. PO21-2F 21
Westmorland Dri. PO22-3A 24
Westmount Caravan Pk. PO20-3B 18
W. Pallant. PO19-3E 7
W. Ridings. BN16-3E 29
W. Sands Caravan Pk. PO20-3A 18
W. Sands La. PO20-4A 18
W. Stoke Rd. PO18 & PO19-3A 2
West St. PO19-3D 6
West St. PO20-5B 18
West St. PO21-6D 22
W. View Dri. BN18-6F 9
W. Walberton La. BN18-1G 9
West Wlk. BN16-4E 29
Westward Clo. PO18-4C 4
Westward Ho. PO19-3A 6
Westway. BN17-6E 13
West Way. PO19-3H 5
(Fishbourne)
West Way. PO19-5A 2
(West Broyle)
Westway. PO22-3E 23
Whapple, The. BN17-3A 28
Wharf Rd. BN17-2E 27
Wheatcroft. BN17-6E 13
Wheatfield Rd. PO20-3E 19
Whistler Av. PO19-6E 3
White Acre. BN17-6E 13
Whitebeam Way. PO22-3D 24
Whitecroft. BN17-2C 28
White Horse Caravan Pk. PO20-3C 18
White Horses Way. BN17-2A 28
White Knights Av. PO21-4D 22
Whitelands. PO22-2H 23
Whitelea Rd. BN17-1F 27
White Rose Touring Pk. BN17-4F 13
Whiteside Clo. PO19-2F 7
Whiteways. PO22-2B 22
Whiteways Clo. BN17-1F 27
Whiteways Clo. PO22-2B 22
Whitfield Clo. PO22-3F 23
Whyke Clo. PO19-5F 7
Whyke Ct. PO19-5F 7
Whyke La. PO19-3F 7
(in two parts)
Whyke Rd. PO19-5F 7
Wick Clo. PO22-4A 24
Wick Farm Rd. BN17-1E 27
Wick La. PO22-4A 24
Wick Pde. BN17-6F 13
Wick St. BN17-1F 27
Widgeon Clo. PO20-3A 18
William Rd. PO19-3H 7
Williams Rd. PO18-2C 4
William St. PO21-5E 23
Willow Av. BN16-2E 29
Willowbed Av. PO19-5G 7
Willowbed Dri. PO19-5G 7
Willow Brook. BN17-6E 13
Willow Ct. PO19-3B 6
Willowhale Av. PO21-3F 21
Willowhayne Av. BN16-3G 29
Willowhayne Cres. BN16-3G 29
Willows Caravan Site. PO20-5B 8
Willows, The. BN16-2D 28
Willows, The. PO20-3D 18
Willow Way. PO21-4D 20
Wilman Gdns. PO21-3F 21
Wilson Clo. PO19-2B 6
Wilton Clo. PO20-6H 17
Winchester Dri. PO19-1D 6
Winchester Rd. BN16-1E 29
Winden Av. PO19-3F 7
Windlesham Gdns. BN16-1G 29
Windmill Clo. PO21-4D 20
Windmill Ct. PO20-4E 17
Windmill Dri. BN16-1D 28
Windmill Field. PO18-4A 4
Windmill Rd. BN17-4F 27
Windsor Clo. PO21-1G 21
Windsor Dri. BN16-6B 14
Windsor Dri. PO20-4D 16
Windsor Rd. PO19-3G 7
Windsor Rd. PO20-5D 18
Windward Clo. BN17-2A 28
Winston Clo. PO21-2A 22

Winston Cres. PO21-2A 22
Winterbourne Rd. PO19-5E 3
Winter Knoll, The. BN17-2H 27
Wiston Av. PO19-5C 6
Wolsey Sq. PO21-4D 20
Wolstenbury Rd. BN16-6D 14
Woodbridge Pk. BN16-2G 29
Woodcote La. BN17-4F 13
Woodend. PO21-4B 22
Woodfield Clo. PO21-6C 20
Woodgate Clo. PO20-4A 8
Woodgate Pk. PO20-3A 8
Woodgate Rd. PO20-4A 8
Woodland Rd. PO20-6C 18
Woodlands Av. BN16-2C 28
Woodlands Clo. BN16-2G 15
  (Angmering)

Woodlands Clo. BN16-1C 28
  (Rustington)
Woodlands Cotts. BN16-1C 28
Woodlands La. PO19-1D 6
Woodlands Pk. Caravan Site. BN18-5F 9
Woodlands Rd. BN17-3G 27
Woodlands Rd. PO22-2C 22
Woodruff Bus. Cen. PO19-4C 6
Woodside. PO22-3E 9
Wood St. PO21-6C 22
Wood View. BN18-5C 10
Woolsteps, The. PO19-3D 6
Worcester Clo. PO21-2G 21
Worcester Rd. PO19-6D 2
Wordsworth Gdns. PO22-3C 24
Worms La. PO22-2B 24
  (in two parts)

Worthing Rd. BN16-1F 29
Worthing Rd. BN17 & BN16-6F 13
Wren Cres. PO22-2C 22
Wren Way. BN17-5E 13
Wroxham Way. PO22-2G 23
Wyatt Ct. PO20-4E 17
Wych Wood Clo. PO21-4F 21
Wychwood Wlk. PO21-4G 21
Wyde Feld. PO21-6A 22
Wyke La. N. PO22-3B 24
Wythering Clo. PO21-6B 20

Yapton La. BN18-1H 9
Yapton Rd. BN18-2E 25
  (Bilsham)

Yapton Rd. BN18-6H 9
  (Yapton)
Yapton Rd. PO22-4F 9
  (Barnham)
Yapton Rd. PO22-4D 24
  (Middleton)
Yeomans Acre. PO21-5A 22
Yew Tree Clo. PO22-2C 22
York Chase. PO19-5D 2
York Gdns. BN17-2F 27
York Rd. BN17-2F 27
York Rd. PO19-4G 7
York Rd. PO20-6D 18
York Rd. PO21-5E 23
Young St. PO19-6E 3

D. M. E. FRENCH
104 Upper Brighton Rd
Worthing
West Sussex BN14 9HR
01903-234144